BARNEY BARNES

BORN TO BE A WARRIOR

Fight with Passion!

Barney Barnes

1 John 3:16

Copyright © 2011 John R. "Barney" Barnes, CDR USN (Ret.)
BORN TO BE A WARRIOR
Printed in the USA

ISBN: 978-0-9846311-8-6
Library of Congress Control Number: 2011941302

All Rights Reserved. No part of this publication may be produced or transmitted in any form or by any means without written permission of the author. The author guarantees all contents are original and do not infringe upon the legal rights of any other person or work.

Prepared for Publication By

Palm Tree Publications is a Division of Palm Tree Productions
www.palmtreeproductions.com
PO BOX 122 | KELLER, TX | 76244

All Scripture quotations are marked:

Scripture taken from the HOLY BIBLE, NEW INTERNATIONAL VERSION ®. Copyright © 1973, 1978, 1984 Biblica. Used by permission of Zondervan. All rights reserved.

Scripture quotations taken from the Amplified® Bible, Copyright © 1954, 1958, 1962, 1964, 1965, 1987 by The Lockman Foundation. La Habra, CA. Used by permission.

Scripture taken from The Message ®. Copyright © 1993, 1994, 1995, 1996, 2000, 2001, 2002. Used by permission of NavPress Publishing Group. Colorado Springs, CO. All rights reserved.

Scripture taken from the New King James Version (NKJV) of the Bible. Copyright © 1982 by Thomas Nelson, Inc. Used by permission. All rights reserved.

To Contact the Author:
Email: borntobeawarrior63@yahoo.com

DEDICATION

To my wonderful parents,
Rev. E. W. "Shorty" Barnes
and
Dorothy Irlene Barnes,
who gave me life,
roots, and wings...

and

to my wonderful wife
Pat, my bride of 42
summers,
my "ezer kenegdo."
(my lifesaver)

Born to be a Warrior

ENDORSEMENTS

Born To Be a Warrior is a masterfully written manual for seasoned, as well as, aspiring Christian warriors. I have known Barney Barnes for over 20 years, both as a Navy Commander and Chief Deputy Sheriff. In all cases he was first of all a cherished Christian brother and secondly a fearless warrior leader. By example, he inspired other leaders to press on---mean what you say and say what you mean---pay the price---finish what you start---depend on God! This manual is all about application and action and should be studied and conveniently located for every Christian warrior's ready reference.

Jimmy S. Gallant
Vicar, St. Paul's Episcopal Church Orangeburg, SC; Senior Chaplain, Charleston Police Department; Former City Councilman, Charleston, SC

Barney Barnes has fanned into flame the spark of "warriorship" that resides in the heart of every Christian boy and man. Through clever analogies, historical facts, and hard-hitting Biblical principles, *Born To Be a Warrior* takes the Christian male on an inspirational journey to reconnect with his "warrior DNA". A must read for every spiritual warrior who seeks to fulfill God's call to battle "against the spiritual forces of evil in the heavenly realms."

Sheriff Ray Nash, (Ret)
President, Police Dynamics Institute

BORN TO BE A WARRIOR

There are two profound truths that I have come to acknowledge in nearly 35 years of ministry to men. (1) We, as men, are engaged in a life struggle; there is an enemy who is set on our destruction. (2) God has given to each of us all that is necessary to be victorious! A warrior spirit and faithful brothers to provide accountability and affirmation will certainly provide for our ultimate victory. With skill and spiritual maturity, Barney Barnes has provided a well researched and thoughtful work, *Born To Be a Warrior*. This warrior's manual reflects his personal knowledge and God revealed insight for every man's spiritual battle. I'm hopeful every pastor and church men's group will take full advantage of this serious work and a great shout of victory will be ours!

Dr. Rick Kingham
President, The Center For Global Leadership; Former Vice President, Promise Keepers; Former President, National Coalition of Ministries to Men

---

Commander Barney Barnes, USN, (Ret), has captured the essence of the Father's purpose for His sons in *Born To Be a Warrior*. He skillfully provokes his reader to acknowledge that Almighty God, has had and continues to have, a divine and declared purpose for His sons. The life breath of the Supreme Creator is to affirm His plan and purpose of making man in His own image: A WARRIOR! I highly recommend that men wear out these pages of insight, truth, and anointed wisdom from one that has served in combat both for his country and for his King.

Rev. Rick Lindsay
Founder, Encourage Men to Pray Ministries; Prayer Director, National Coalition of Ministries to Men; Prayer Coordinator, National Day of Prayer, South Carolina

Endorsements

Commander Barnes is all warrior, all man, and all God's. Though primarily written to men, I believe this book should be read by youth and all men and women who desire to understand the warfare of the Kingdom. Barnes takes transferrable concepts and principles from his knowledge as a military strategist, from his real life warfare experiences, and from the warriors who served with him. The famous generals of history such as Sun Tzu, Von Clausewitz, Genghis Khan, Napoleon and Alexander the Great articulated man's natural art of warfare. Commander Barnes takes that to the high level of the art of spiritual warfare and uncovers the mentality, the heart, and the mission of God's spiritual warriors. *Born to Be a Warrior* is a "mind blower" and a "heart exploder" for those called to such a band of brothers. This is the must read of the year.

John P. Kelly
Convening Apostle of the International Coalition of Apostles; CEO of LEAD

Commander Barnes has struck gold in writing this warrior's manual. It is a timely call for all Christian men to "man up" and find their positions in the ranks. Born To Be a Warrior has challenged me in every area of my life as a Christian man--- husband, father, church elder and college administrator. I have been inspired to allow the warrior spirit to be unleashed from within me to contend in the spiritual darkness in the culture around us. In so doing the ultimate warrior, Jesus Christ, can emerge through me and draw others to Him. This is a much needed work and I salute it wholeheartedly.

Lt. Col. Justin H. Pearson, Sr. SCM
Senior Associate Director of Admissions, The Citadel

Born to be a Warrior

In a feminized world that calls men to be passive and weak, Barney Barnes has given men a manual for Godly manhood. It is fresh, clear, readable, and applicable for men of all ages. This is a road map for men to become the warriors God created us to be and to raise up the next generation of men in God's image. When you are ready to start becoming the man God intended for you to be, this book should be your training manual.

Dr. Chuck Stecker
President/Founder, A Chosen Generation; Lt. Colonel (Ret) US Army Ranger, Special Forces; Former, Regional Director, Promise Keepers

---

Spiritual warfare started in heaven between Father God and Satan, long before we mortals were created, in order to understand the warfare on Earth. Like it or not, we become a part of this spiritual warfare by virtue of our relationship to Father God through Jesus Christ. This manual will train the spiritual warrior in the art of spiritual war, how to properly engage the battle, and how to win with a band of brothers.

Dr. Edward L. Johnson
Pastor, Friendship Inspirational Church of God in Christ, Lincolnville, SC; Director, Millennium IMPACT Conferences

---

Barney Barnes is a true warrior, having served his country as a career naval officer and combat aviator, and having served his community in the sheriff's office as Chief of Staff. Drawing from these rich experiences, Barney helps men understand how we all are "born to be warriors." This book is a great tool that will help men of all ages understand our spiritual calling to fight for what matters most. Barney not only helps us understand this, he provides some very practical insights that help us step up and actually get into the battle.

Rick Caldwell
Director of Authentic Manhood/Men's Fraternity

Endorsements

So much that is written on spiritual warfare today is more philosophical than theological. *Born To Be a Warrior* is definitely not in that category. I've had the pleasure of knowing Commander Barney Barnes for over 22 years, initially where he served as an elder in a church that we helped establish. Barney's love for God and the people of God were clearly demonstrated as well as his passion to see the kingdom of darkness be humiliated in its efforts to capture the inheritance that belongs to the Church. Much of my understanding of spiritual warfare has come through this warrior's understanding. He skillfully develops the practical application of biblical illustrations and concepts and demonstrates their seamless relationship to natural war and spiritual war. If you are serious about confronting and dealing with spiritual darkness then this warrior's manual is a must read and study guide.

Keith Tucci
Founding Pastor, Living Hope Church, Whitney, Pa ; Senior Apostle, Network of Related Pastors

---

At a time when many cultural influences demean manhood and fatherhood, *Born To Be a Warrior* sets men firmly on Biblical ground. It helps to fill the void between the culture's diluted projection of manhood and the manhood God has intended. Edmund Burke reminded us, "All that is necessary for evil to triumph is for good men to do nothing." In this manual for warriors Barney Barnes has given men a road map for triumphing over evil as a band of brothers.

John Hull
Chairman, The Summerville 912 Project

BORN TO BE A WARRIOR

Warfare, both natural and spiritual, can be a dangerous place even for well equipped and disciplined warriors. Barney's exploits with the Seawolves reveals great insight into spiritual warfare dynamics. My Vietnam experiences involved, special warfare missions in which the warrior spirit Barney speaks off was vital to success. When we finally met in 1989, both of us were committed Christians and teamed up under the leadership of Apostle John P. Kelly. We became aware that the spiritual warfare arena is just as real as the natural warfare arena, the one we were most familiar with. *Born To Be a Warrior*, an authentic warriors manual, was greatly needed then and even more so now. I highly recommend that each man devour its contents and disseminate them wherever God assigns him.

R. L. "Dutch" Scheierman, LCDR, USN (Ret)

John "Barney" Barnes is one of my heroes. In *Born To Be a Warrior* he very well articulates what many of us believe and feel, the warrior spirit. The people of God are called to be warrior princes (and princesses) in the Kingdom of God. It is vital that we be the people of "good courage" during these challenging times. This warrior's manual will inspire and equip you to be that warrior that confronts and overcomes the demonic forces arrayed against you and those you love.

William N. Gadol
President, Government Marketing International, Inc

Endorsements

Great work and even greater read! *Born To Be a Warrior* has really stirred and renewed my spiritual fighting spirit. Barney Barnes led me, and my family, to a faith in Jesus Christ when he was a navy commander and I was on a professional staff on Capitol Hill some 25 years ago. Spiritual warfare can be very intense around centers of political power and this manual reveals the secret to winning these battles, even on Capitol Hill. I have been a beneficiary of these principles and they have enabled me to successfully challenge Congressional leaders on many occasions to take stands for righteousness in the legislative arena. This manual is your plan to be victorious over evil and to guide, direct, and enable the next generation of holy warriors. As we say on Capitol Hill, "this the real deal."

John H. Forehand
Vice President, CF Federal, LLC; Former Congressional Committee, Senior Professional Staff; Past President, Capitol Hill Chapter Full Gospel Businessmen's Fellowship International ;

Born To Be a Warrior comes at an incredible time for me as a Christian husband and father of 4 children. This manual not only gives me a personal warrior path but also clearly shows how to nurture warrior qualities into my son. The culture is at war against the family and particularly any father who may stand up for Christian values. Mr. Barnes has fused God's Word with his real life examples and personal history to offer simple instruction to anyone wise enough to pick up this book, read it, and follow what it says. Don't wait another day. Get this warrior manual, read it, and begin applying it now!

Craig Corbin
IT Senior Executive, World Wide Technology, Inc

BORN TO BE A WARRIOR

Victory is always on the other side of a fight. Don't live life as roadkill, get this book and gird up your loins. Let Barney Barnes take you on the adventure of your life. He's not just talking, he lived this... learn from the best and live the life you've always desired.

Paul Louis Cole

President, Christian Men's Network Worldwide;
Author, "Daring: A Call to Courageous Manhood"

Barney's masterful blending of warrior insights from Xenophon to Schwarzkopf with Biblical truths from Jesus Christ is by far the best I have ever seen. At Troy State University *Born To Be a Warrior* will enrich the lives of many young men who will become great leaders, as well as many young women who need to understand the warrior spirit in these men. I will use this book, teach from this book, and share the book with others.

John A. Kline, PhD

Distinguished Professor
Director of the Institute for Leadership Development, Troy University

---

Born To Be a Warrior is a stirring and timely call to action for a Christian culture that needs to hear this message. Barney has artfully crafted a manual that has equipped and encouraged me to have a warrior mentality against evil, with the servant, loving heart of Christ.

Allan E. Parker, J.D

Founder and President, The Justice Foundation

Contents

Acknowledgements	xix
Foreword by Willam G. "Jerry" Boykin, LTG (Ret)	xxiii
Introduction	1

Part 1: Born to be a Warrior — 17

1. The Quest—The Fellowship of Arms — 19
2. The Dream in Every Little Boy's Heart — 25
3. Defining the Warrior Code — 33
4. The Samurai, the Knight and Jesus — 37
5. David and the Warrior Spirit — 45
6. The Warrior Spirit in Modern Culture — 53

Part 1 Study Guide — 59
   Thoughts for Reflection
   or Group Discussion

Part 2: The Warrior Spirit — 63

7. The Origin of the Warrior Spirit DNA — 65
8. Piercing the Spiritual Darkness with Night Fighters — 69
9. Owning the Night — 73

10. My Personal Passage Into the Fellowship of Arms	75
11. The World of the Seawolves	77
12. Seawolf Principles of Warfare	87
13. Getting Out of Binh Thuy	101
14. Fire From the Sky	103
15. Who Will Own the Night?	107

PART 2 STUDY GUIDE   113
    Thoughts for Reflection
    or Group Discussion

PART 3: THE WARRIOR IN ACTION/ WARRIOR QUALITIES   117

16. The Proper Exercise of Authority	119
17. The Warrior and His Sword	131
18. The Warrior and His Integrity	147
19. The Warrior and His Honor	159
20. The Warrior and His Loyalty	169
21. The Warrior and His Courage	179

PART 3 STUDY GUIDE   189
    Thoughts for Reflection
    or Group Discussion

Table of Contents

Part 4: Warrior Leadership and Warrior Values — 193
- 22. The Warrior as a Leader: — 195
- 23. The Lionship of Leadership — 203
- 24. The Warrior and His Core Values — 209
- 25. Creeds, Oaths and the Warrior Spirit — 217

Part 4 Study Guide — 223
Thoughts for Reflection or Group Discussion

Part 5: Warfare Theory and Practice — 225
- 26. Center of Gravity — 227
- 27. The Nine Principles of War — 239
- 28. War Cries and Shouts — 255

Part 5 Study Guide — 261
Thoughts for Reflection or Group Discussion

Part 6: Songs of War and The Warrior's Prayer — 263
- 29. Onward Christian Soldiers — 265
- 30. A Warrior's Prayer — 271

Born to be a Warrior

ACKNOWLEDGEMENTS

I have been blessed by God with a life of challenge and adventure. As a bonus I have shared it with the most wonderful people in the whole world, beginning with my parents, Rev. E.W. "Shorty" and Dorothy Irlene Barnes who loved me unconditionally. They brought me up in rural East Tennessee in the "nurture and admonition of the Lord" and gave me the best gifts that any parents can give…roots and wings.

Then God gave me my *ezer kenegdo,* my "lifesaver," as John Eldredge emphasizes in his classic for men *Wild at Heart.* Patricia has been my lovely bride for 41 summers. We were married by an Army chaplain, in a Navy wedding with my shipmates, at Fort Rucker Alabama, just one month before I left for a year in Vietnam. Pat has truly been my "lifesaver" on numerous occasions and has always made me feel complete and whole as a man.

Along the way several warriors have had a profound effect in shaping and disciplining me in the fellowship of arms and in the fellowship of faith. Barry Spofford, who led me back to Christ, a warrior and my commanding officer—his life and testimony changed mine. The great warrior, Dr. Edwin Louis Cole, significantly impacted my life with his anointed ministry called Christian Men's Network, that continues to impact the nations.

Born to be a Warrior

I had the good fortune to serve under two Admirals who had been Prisoners of War for over five years. These warriors, both men of faith, brought a unique perspective to Navy leadership. I was molded by William P. Lawrence and Byron J. Fuller and their genuine love of country, reverence for the sacred, and the warrior spirit with which they served.

There are many faithful brothers, especially R.L. "Dutch" Scheierman and John Henry Forehand. Dutch was a special ops type warrior in the Navy and taught me much about spiritual warfare and fighting demonic forces. I had the great honor of leading John to a faith in Jesus Christ when I served in Washington DC. John was a very well connected lobbyist and afterwards assisted me in getting a Navy-wide prison program fully funded.

I have had the honor of serving with and under several elders, pastors and apostles on my quest. Pastor Bob Yarbrough and Apostle John Kelly were especially formative, providing an authority covering and encouragement for my spiritual growth. Larry Burgbacher, my current pastor at Faith Assembly of God in Summerville, South Carolina, has blessed my life with his warrior spirit, integrity and sincere encouragement for me to write.

In my final professional capacity, I had the great honor and pleasure to serve as Chief of Staff for Sheriff Ray Nash. He refreshed my appreciation

Acknowledgements

for the Constitution and with virtue and integrity demonstrated the true warrior spirit while he served as a South Carolina Sheriff. At this writing he serves his country with courage and distinction in Afghanistan.

Finally, a major inspiration to actually put this book to print was the living example of courage and faith demonstrated by William G. "Jerry" Boykin, LTG (Ret). I was not really aware of him personally until late in his army career when he served with the Secretary of Defense. I distinctly recall linking him to the special warfare missions that I was very familiar with. His assessment of the nature of Jihad, its spiritual roots, and the real threat this presented to our very way of life "rang true" in my spirit. General Boykin continues to bring great clarity to bear on these issues through his ministy called Kingdom Warriors. General Boykin has certainly inspired me, as a warrior, to write about and for warriors—to be engaged in the culture, and to "press on to the high calling."

—**John R. "Barney" Barnes, CDR USN (Ret.)**
Summerville, South Carolina

Born to be a Warrior

THE NATION THAT MAKES A GREAT DISTINCTION BETWEEN ITS SCHOLARS AND ITS WARRIORS WILL HAVE ITS THINKING DONE BY COWARDS AND ITS FIGHTING DONE BY FOOLS.

–Thucydides (460 BC-395 BC)

FOREWORD

Men in America are struggling with many issues today. The proliferation of pornography, the changing sexual morality, and the pressure to succeed are all issues that create internal strife for men. America's secular society continues to try to convince men that they are no different than women except in their biological composition. They are bombarded with a continual message of equality between men and women. Well, that message is true in a spiritual context as God makes no distinction between the sexes regarding His Love nor His Grace.

However, God has indeed made men to play a different role in the family structure. He created men to be the protector, the provider, the priest, and the professor of the family unit. In his book, *Born To Be a Warrior*, Barney Barnes captures the intent of The Creator in making Man in His own image. Exodus 15:3 says that "The Lord Is A Warrior. The Lord Is His Name." Man was created to be a warrior regardless of the societal norms of the nation today, it is a vital part of his spiritual DNA.

Barney is himself a warrior with many years of experience as a naval officer, combat aviator, and law enforcement official. He understands the meaning of *Warfare* and he understands what it takes to be an effective warrior. As a committed Christian, Barney also knows his enemy, Satan. He has studied the enemy and accepts the biblical teachings of spiritual warfare as a critical issue for men to understand.

Using his own experiences and understanding of biblical teachings on the subject of spiritual warfare and the warrior ethos, Barney has developed the finest guide to understanding and taking effective action that I have seen. He connects the dots between physical and spiritual warfare and demonstrates how the principles of war apply in both realms. He does this while clearly articulating the Godly principle of being a warrior. Men are called to do battle, especially in the spiritual realm, and must be prepared to do so.

This book will be a eureka moment for the reader as it will explain why so many men struggle with a sense of inadequacy regarding their role in society. In short, it is because they are BORN TO BE WARRIORS but they are inundated with a message that conflicts with

Foreword

what God put in their hearts. This book clarifies these very issues that men must know and understand. It is written by a man-of-war who knows what he is writing about ... because he lives it!

William G. "Jerry" Boykin, LTG (Ret)
Executive Vice President, Family Research Council

William G. "Jerry" Boykin, LTG (Ret) U.S. Army Ranger, Special Forces, was serving as United States Deputy Undersecretary of Defense for Intelligence when he retired after 37 years of active duty in 2007. During his illustrious career he played a significant role in most every major military operation of the United States over the past four decades including; Grenada, Somalia, and Iraq. He is the author of *Never Surrender: A Soldiers Journey to the Crossroads of Faith and Freedom* and the founder of Kingdom Warriors Ministry. He is a frequent speaker at national and regional conferences as well as a radio and television guest, speaking to emerging issues of national relevancy. He currently serves as Executive Vice President of the Family Research Council.

Born to Be A Warrior

INTRODUCTION

OUR FATHER GOD IS A WARRIOR—HIS SONS CARRY THE WARRIOR DNA

The LORD is a man of war (milchamah);
the LORD is His name.
—Exodus 15:3 NKJV

DAVID: Praise be to the Lord my Rock,
who trains my hands for war, my
fingers for battle (milchamah).
—Psalm 144:1 NIV

PAUL: Not that I have already attained, or
am already perfected; but I press on,
that I may lay hold of that for which Christ
Jesus has also laid hold of me.
—Philippians 3:12 NKJV

TO GIDEON: The Lord is with you
mighty warrior (gibbor).
—Judges 6:12b NIV

Born To Be A Warrior

God is a warrior! That's amazing when you think about it. He is, of course, our Father God. But our Father God is a man of war as Moses stated above. He has a warrior's heart and so a warrior's spirit. He has placed that 'warrior' spirit into His sons, men created in His image, so they too can become holy warriors. This is an essential component of what I will call Spiritual Warfare Plan A (SWP-A). This is the divinely conceived strategy to defeat the demonic forces of spiritual darkness arrayed against all Believers. As the saying goes, there is no Spiritual Warfare Plan B (SWP-B).

A two word description of SWP-A would be "power projection," which is a military term. Instead of projecting the power of the nation against our enemies, as in conventional warfare, the Church is to project the power of the Cross against these demonic forces. In so doing, we also project the power of God's great love to a fallen world. In short, SWP-A calls for regime change and nation building. Ponder that a moment.

All of the great campaigns in the history of natural war and all of the great spiritual awakenings have witnessed the mobilization of warriors. The account of warriors joining David in 1 Chronicles 12 makes my point very well. *All these men of war, who could keep ranks, came to Hebron with a loyal heart, to make David king over all Israel*, (vs. 38a NKJV). Regime change…nation building…power projection, yes, our God has conquest on His mind. I believe we are entering another such period, and so there is a call for men from headquarters; for holy warriors to

Introduction

report for duty and to "man up." He is calling men of one heart to make Jesus the Lord of all!

My definition of the warrior spirit is a simple one. It is **the passionate desire and determination in the heart of a man to perfect himself for the stance against evil in the service to others.** Throughout history, this heart of self-sacrifice and service to others has been the hallmark of great warrior traditions. The legendary Samurai warriors of Japan, and the Christian knights of medieval times are but two.

> ## Warrior Spirit:
> ### The passionate desire and determination in the heart of a man to perfect himself for the stance against evil in the service to others.

Many of our brave warriors, who serve our nation today, in the both the military and in law enforcement carry this same spirit. It is not a spirit of violence or brutality. It is a spirit of power, of justice, and of right versus wrong. However, we must never lose sight of the fact that the consummate example of the spiritual warrior is Jesus Christ. He is the standard bearer for Christian warriors, the man of action who defines self-sacrifice in the service to others.

BORN TO BE A WARRIOR

We men are all born as male babies. In time we become boys. However, it is God's plan that we physically and spiritually mature into men and become warriors. David, Paul and Gideon, listed above, are all great examples of servants of God who embraced a warrior's spirit. I pray that if you have not already done so, you will as well.

Moses introduces us to the fact that God himself is a warrior. In that triumphant song recorded in Exodus 15, Moses and Miriam proclaim "The Lord is a man of war *(milchamah.)*" Most Christians are comfortable with the concept of God as a Father, and having a father's heart. They are not truly aware that God also has a warrior's heart. Perhaps this partially explains the anemic, ineffective responses of so many Christian men when confronting spiritual darkness, or even when being confronted about their own basic responsibilities.

After serving in a military and a law enforcement culture for almost four decades, I often communicate in military or martial terminology. It is what I call "warrior talk," and I believe you will soon see its usefulness in this manual, if you have not already done so. I will also use the Hebrew terms *milchamah* (man of war) and *gibbor* (mighty warrior) as though they were common English words.

When I do a situational analysis (SA) of Judges 6, I see so many similarities to today's culture. Many men are in hiding. Like Gideon, they are removed from the spiritual battle fields of life, even while the enemy's position is expanding. But listen, God is calling men out just as He

Introduction

did Gideon. I believe the *gibbor* (mighty warrior) spirit is in our DNA, and that many men can and will answer this call, just like Gideon.

I believe that God placed this *milchamah* and this *gibbor* in Adam at creation as part of his spiritual DNA. After all, he was made in the image of God. This spirit was evidently ignored by Adam, and he fell into spiritual darkness. It was also dormant in his son Cain, and he behaved like a spoiled boy. The Lord spoke to Cain at a pivotal time about conquering his adversary, *"sin is crouching at your door; it desires to have you, but you must master it"* (Genesis 4:7b NIV).

This was clearly a call to the warrior spirit within him. Unfortunately, Cain followed his father Adam's example and failed his test to "man up." Does this scenario remind you of a more current father/son episode, perhaps one that you have known personally? The Good News is that you do not have to follow that fallen example. You do not have to deny or ignore the *gibbor* God has placed within you. You are created and destined to be a mighty warrior!

> YOU ARE CREATED AND DESTINED TO BE A MIGHTY WARRIOR.

This manual is intended to assist God's men in overcoming the fallen pattern of manhood. Fortunately, we now have a victorious example in the second Adam, Jesus. We also have the empowerment of the Holy Spirit to carry us through to victory. We are really men without excuse.

Some 30 years ago, I was a seasoned combat aviator and a career naval officer. I started asking myself a compelling set of questions. **"Does the warrior model have a relevant role to play in my Christian faith in modern America?"** If so, "how should the warrior model be properly identified and fully integrated into my Christian universe?" "Is there any functional relationship between King David, the warrior serving the God of Israel, and Paul, the warrior serving the Son of God?" Those and other related questions set me on a quest for answers. I needed affirmation that biblical manhood was a reality, that a warrior spirit was God's desire for men, and that I was born to be a warrior. This manual, *Born to Be a Warrior*, is my report on that quest.

For me the statement by King David, *"who trains my hands for war, my fingers for battle (milchamah),"* is not metaphorical in nature. It is warrior talk! In my own mind, the words of David bring up images of fierce combat, and powerful, fond memories of a special band of brothers who fought "the good fight" in a distant land. You see, I flew a heavily armed helicopter gunship supporting Navy SEAL, Swift Boat, and allied operations in the Vietnam War.

Being a combat pilot requires both hands and all fingers to be well trained and skillfully employed. Both feet, and all their movement must be as well. And of course, all of

Introduction

this must be governed by a cool head. Having a trusted wingman flying the "chopper" next to you demanded the same level of concentration, coupled with absolute trust and confidence in each other.

That phrase from King David, even now raises memories of leading an air strike against enemy forces in support of friendly forces.

"My right thumb involuntarily goes slowly up and down as I gently grip the imaginary flight control, the stick in aviator talk. At just the right moment, my thumb carefully depresses the top right red button, launching 2.75 inch rockets into an enemy position. My right index finger squeezes inward, pulling the red trigger switch, actuating the mini guns, laying down 7.62 mm gunfire into that same enemy position, at 4000 rounds per minute in roaring 3 second bursts.

"I also remember the fearless door gunners, whose hands and fingers had also been trained for war, as they commence their contribution to this rain of fire, lighting up the night with .50 cal. and 7.62 mm mini guns."

That was a real shooting war, you say, but what about now? Spiritual war is not like that—or is it?

In spiritual warfare we don't fire mini guns and rockets at the enemy to be sure. However, the demanding training (discipleship), the exacting skills (from practice), and the trust-based relationships (forged in the heat of the battle) are all essentials for both the natural and spiritual warrior to prevail. The principles of war, discussed in a later chapter, have remained mostly constant from the days of Joshua and Sun Tzu to the present.

For many years, Philippians 3:4-17 has been one of my "go to" passages when facing adversity, both spiritual and otherwise. The phrases, "pressing on" and "laying hold of" have a martial flavor. "Not that I have been made perfect," always gave me hope that I could overcome my own shortcomings. "Pressing on toward the goal to win the prize" identified the tempo, the commitment trajectory and the specific goals that stirred my core and the warrior spirit, the *milchamah* and *gibbor,* implanted deep within me by my Father God.

The Apostle Paul had a warrior spirit and spoke warrior talk. More importantly his actions demonstrated his passion for preparing himself for self-sacrifice in the service of Jesus Christ. He wrote of the cost of serving his fellow man, and of his personal mission to conquer the onslaught of satanic forces. It was Paul who boldly said "follow my example as I follow the example of Christ." That is warrior talk!

OUR CULTURE IS IN DESPERATE NEED OF MEN WHO WILL COME OUT OF THE SHADOWS AND MAN UP.

Our culture is in desperate need of such men, men who will come out of the shadows and man up. Jesus, like the Marines, continues to look

Introduction

for "a few good men" to follow Him— "marching as to war" as the old hymn, *Onward Christian Soldiers* rings out so clearly.

I began to gain clarity on my basic questions in the mid 1980s, while serving as a staff officer in Washington DC. My duties included writing position papers, a task I thoroughly enjoyed. I also found myself writing some Christian articles for local publication. These primarily challenged Christians to get involved in the culture around them. If I could summarize my thinking at that time, it would be, **"why don't we take what we talk about on Sunday and do it where we work on Monday?"** Pretty radical huh? I was about to be challenged to do just that.

During this time I became an elder and the men's ministry leader at a new church plant. This was called New Covenant Fellowship (NCF) in Manassas, Virginia, a church which grew to about 1200 members. I understood that my pastor, Bob Yarbrough, was my spiritual covering. I also understood that I went out from NCF to my ministry field, the Navy. Through my prayer time, it became quite clear to me that God had placed me in my Navy position. I was assigned to be Head, Navy Corrections and was amazed that God could work through the Navy bureaucracy. I finally realized that He also had called my wife and I to help plant NCF. I thought that was pretty cool—still do.

God instilled a vision in me to totally rebuild and restructure the antiquated and disconnected Navy Correctional System. When I was assigned to lead Navy

Corrections, the Navy had the capacity to house about 2000 prisoners in 21 shore brigs. These stretched from Guam in the Pacific Ocean to Rota, Spain on the western shore of the Atlantic. No one had a handle on the total cost associated with this operation, and no definable mission had been established to administrate these widely diverse facilities. God's plan, I believed, was to replace the existing system with a modern, integrated system.

I believed that we could implement a total program for the total person, body mind and spirit. I believed that we could have productive prison industries and dynamic prisoner programs. I believed that we could create a challenging and meaningful command environment for military and civilian staff, and do all of this with 15% fewer staff. I believed that our Navy brigs could become more like lighthouses, signaling a safe harbor for repairs, and less like warehouses, providing storage for row upon row of boxes.

The Navy is a very conservative organization, and is more focused on funding ships, airplanes, submarines, and support facilities, and personnel to operate them than it is on restoring broken sailors to productive lives. However, after about 3 years and a series of mighty miracles, we had developed the plan I envisioned. We had obtained approval from the Department of the Navy to proceed, and the Congress had appropriated $70 million to implement that comprehensive plan.

Introduction

The normal Washington D.C. tour would have been three years, followed by rotation back to sea duty. For me that would have meant assignment to an aircraft carrier. I had already been extended two years to complete the Brig Project, so my detailer (assignment officer) was more than eager to get me back to sea. However, my God had other plans and my detailer was overruled once again.

To my great joy, I soon received orders to supervise the building of a new $15 million facility at Charleston, SC, and become its first Commanding Officer. I found a tremendous level of satisfaction knowing that **I had taken what we talked about on Sunday and brought it to where I worked on Monday.**

Born to be a Warrior was in my spirit in those days. It was just not fully developed. I had become convinced that being a Christian and a warrior were mutually inclusive, and I intended to live that way. My discovery of the Christian Men's Network (CMN) and the great warrior Dr. Edwin Louis Cole, around 1986, served to confirm my conviction even more. I actually had the great pleasure of meeting Dr. Cole, and he gave me several "red foot lockers" full of books and teaching tapes to distribute in Navy brigs. Books like *Maximized Manhood* and *Courage* have had a great influence on countless men around the world. I was overwhelmed by his generosity and his compassion for men.

Later, while in Charleston for a CMN conference in 1989, Dr. Cole was kind enough to visit the site of the new facility, which was under construction. After our "hard hat tour" we came back to where my office was being constructed and he prayed with me and prophesied over me. Those moments continue to resonate in my spirit more than 22 years later, as the words he spoke then unfold in my life, even as I write this manual.

After Dr. Cole's inspirational visit, I developed the command motto, "Bearing the Standard For Correctional Excellence." Following our fourth year of operations we requested an Accreation Audit by the American Correctional Association covering 448 national standards. The command scored an amazing 100%, a feat virtually unprecedented on initial accreation. The command has since scored 100% on seven of these tri-annual audits. Over time, "Bearing The Standard for Correctional Excellence" became more than a motto, it became our unit identity and the national standard.

At about this same time I met another great warrior, Apostle John P. Kelly. The thrust of His ministry clearly demonstrated that the warrior spirit had relevance for the modern Church. The concept of a vibrant New Testament type of church was both refreshing and instructive. I saw first-hand that men could be trained for spiritual warfare, much as they are trained for natural warfare. My vision and inspiration for this manual is rooted in that era.

I remember Apostle Kelly saying that while "Moses generally protected the people from danger; it was Joshua who prepared the people to face danger." I saw

Introduction

authentic models of church activity which reflected a "Joshua mind set" more than that of Moses. The church was not designed by God to be a spiritual hospital only. Rather it was ordained to be a fighting battalion with a "field hospital" component. It was never the purpose to be a stationary building filled with well-trained, but unproven recruits. Sadly, many churches are just that, safe training encampments with no real offensive component. They offer no significant strategic or tactical threat to the demonic forces of darkness.

> *"Strategy without tactics is the slowest route to victory. Tactics without strategy is the noise before defeat."*
> -Sun Tzu (544 BC-496 BC) - The Art of War

My desire is also to quicken the route to victory and eliminate the noise level before defeat for our men in their spiritual warfare encounters. When I was a combat pilot I studied the aircraft manual relentlessly (we called it "the bible"). I also spent a lot of time studying the tactics manual. These manuals were not designed to be read and put aside. They were to be kept close at hand for study, reference and discussion. This manual is meant to be a similar guide, coupled with your "flight manual"—your Bible.

For most of the last 40 years I have worn a warrior suit of one type or another. I have been an officer in the U.S. Navy, a husband, a combat pilot, a deacon, a father and grandfather, a prayer leader, a South Carolina State

Guard Battalion Commander, a church elder, a chief deputy sheriff, and a men's group leader. **During these four decades, I have come to see a seamless association between natural and spiritual war and the principles that govern both.**

If you have a desire to become a warrior, or assist other men to become warriors, or if you just want to become a more effective warrior yourself, then this manual is for you. You will see how being made in the image of God includes having the warrior spirit DNA as part of your makeup. *Milchamah* and *gibbor* will become a tangible part of your standard of Christian experience. You will also discover, or perhaps re-discover, the concept that becoming a warrior is a process, a life-style governed by a passion of the heart, a desire to prepare yourself to stand against evil in the service to others.

This manual is unlike any other you will find. It includes sections on warfare theory such as the Nine Principles of War and Center of Gravity; subject matter Christian authors do not usually address. I have also included significant essays written for warriors on leadership, integrity, loyalty, core values, courage, honor, warrior and weapon relationships, war cries and shouts, and the proper exercise of authority. At the end is A Warrior's Prayer, a confident assertion of reliance on God—the Warrior, to prepare, establish, and sustain you as a man of war, a *milchamah* and a *gibbor*. All of these are rooted in my life experiences, great warriors in the history of natural warfare, and various warriors in the Bible.

Introduction

The life of a warrior is a life of training, preparation and adherence to specific disciplines. This pattern of discipline is essential in order for the spiritual warrior or the natural warrior to be viable and effective in battle. The writer of Hebrews reminds us *"but God disciplines us for our good that we may share in his holiness. No discipline seems pleasant at the time, but painful. Later on, however, it produces a harvest of righteousness and peace for those who have been trained by it."* (Hebrews 12:10b-11 NIV).

> THE LIFE OF A WARRIOR IS A LIFE OF TRAINING, PREPARATION, AND ADHERENCE TO SPECIFIC DISCIPLINES.

As men, we can desire to learn and acquire the skill sets necessary to operate as effective, spiritual warriors, not unlike the Samurai and medieval knights of old. A more understandable model would be the courageous men and women who serve in our nation's military and law enforcement ranks today. They are the ever vigilant warriors, that "long gray line," who defend the nation, often in foreign lands; and that "thin blue line," who serve and faithfully protect us in our homeland, around the clock.

It is their oath of office that affirms in part, *"that I will support and defend the Constitution of the United States against all enemies, foreign and domestic, that I will bear true faith and allegiance to the same; that I take this obligation freely, without any mental reservation or purpose of evasion; and that I will well and faithfully discharge the duties of the office upon which I am about to enter."*

I think most Christian men would like to somehow become identified with such a warrior code and noble tradition. In reality we can be, just not in those terms. The writer of Hebrews tells us in chapter 12 that *we are surrounded by such a great cloud of witnesses*. To me, this speaks of the most glorious of traditions, and what I will call the "eternal red line." We will discuss all this in some detail in THE WARRIOR CODE, in Part I of this manual.

To be a warrior one must first have a pure heart. King David surely knew well of this basic requirement when he cried out, *"Create in me a pure heart, O God, and renew a steadfast spirit within me."* (Psalm 51:10 NIV). Having established this prerequisite one must train like a warrior, think like a warrior, behave like a warrior and speak the language of warriors. In this regard, it is like learning to speak a foreign language while in a foreign country. However, you will either use it or lose it, just as Cain did.

> For though we live in the world,
> we do not wage war as the world does.
> The weapons we fight with are not the
> weapons of the world. On the contrary they
> have divine power to demolish strongholds.
> —2 Corinthians 10:3-4 (NIV)

PART ONE

BORN TO BE A WARRIOR

BORN TO BE A WARRIOR

Do not, nor slay not, anything that will dishonor the fair name of Christian knighthood for only by stainless and honorable lives, not by prowess and courage (alone), will the final goal be reached. Therefore be a good knight and so I pray to God, so ye may be and if you be of prowess and worthiness then ye shall be a Knight of the Round Table.

—King Arthur's Charge to His Knights

Chapter 1

THE QUEST— THE FELLOWSHIP OF ARMS

Above all else, guard your heart, for everything you do flows from it.
—Proverbs 4:23 (NIV)

In war, the only sure defense is offense, and the efficiency of the offense depends upon the warlike souls of those conducting it.
—General George S. Patton (1885-1945)

I do not believe that a man is born a warrior, either in a martial or spiritual context. However, I do believe that a man is born to be a warrior as a result of being made in the image of God. Consequently, becoming a warrior is a process. It is a becoming and a transformation, with no guarantees of success.

After much study and observation in the arena of life, I believe the true warrior spirit can be described in very simple and easy to understand terms. The warrior spirit is **the passionate desire and determination in the heart of**

Part 1—Born To Be A Warrior

a man, a desire to perfect himself for the stance against evil in the service to others. It is this warrior spirit, not positive mental attitude or braggadocio that empowers, and even compels a man to perform selfless, often sacrificial acts, in the service to others. More often than not, these deeds, guided by the warrior spirit, are done without regard for personal convenience, and in some cases without regard for personal safety.

Culturally speaking, I have been a member of the warrior class most of my adult life. My professional journey began as a naval officer and combat aviator in 1969 and ended as a law enforcement official in 2009. It seems that in one form or another, the bad guys have always been the target in my crosshairs.

Of note is a seminal event that occurred 1981, when I made a personal decision to make Jesus the Lord of my life. From that point I began a quest to be a more effective natural warrior, as well as a more effective spiritual warrior. I am still on active duty in the Lord's Army and on the quest of perfecting myself for the service to others. Over this period of time I have come to view the natural and spiritual order as virtually seamless with regard to the governing laws and principles of warfare. In this manual we will explore these concepts extensively.

Starting about 1983, I made another decision, to be careful not to put on a "work face" approaching my professional duties, and a "church face" or a "home face" approaching those duties. In a very practical way this gave me a more wholesome view of myself, less of a "fractionalized man" and more of being a whole man. My goal was to be an undivided man. The "who I was" began to take precedent over the "what I do."

It has been my experience that a man, influenced by culture, can allow himself to be defined by his position. This makes him more prone to being self-absorbed. **The less secure a man is the more prevalent this seems to be.** Jesus was not such a man. He was totally aware of who He was and that governed what He did. *Who, being in the form of God…But made of Himself no reputation, taking the form of a bondservant…*Philippians 2:6a,7a (NKJV). I call this new approach to life that I discovered "Jesusesque," in other words how our Lord did it. I have yet to meet a man who has heard the term "Jesusesque," but it may just catch on.

Along the way, I have encountered and dealt with some very evil and dangerous people. I have also confronted some very evil spiritual forces, often at the same time. When good confronts evil, I believe it is God's plan for good to prevail. The crime scene of the first homicide, Genesis 4:8, is a case in point. God saw Cain's anger and warned him, *sin is crouching at your door; it desires to have you, but you must master it.* In Cain's case evil prevailed, but that was clearly not God's plan for Cain.

Cain is a real good example of an adult male whose thoughts and actions were those of a boy. We men are all born males. But just like Cain, all males do not become

Part 1—Born To Be A Warrior

men. Sadly, I have encountered countless males, from 18 to 60 years of age, whose thoughts and actions were those of boys, not men—just like Cain. Although many of these encounters have been in a law enforcement capacity, many others have been in various areas throughout our culture to include church life.

American culture often contradicts God's plan for boys to become men. This makes becoming a warrior very difficult. Historically, the rise of effeminate males in any culture is telling evidence of the decline of that culture. Witness the Roman Empire, for example. There has been growing evidence of that in America, across several decades, with what I call the "Phil Donahue effect." The recent repeal of the Department of Defense's policy on homosexuality, and attempts to redefine marriage are cause for genuine concern.

> American culture often contradicts God's plan for boys to become men.

Throughout history, and in virtually all cultures, we can recognize an established process for training young men, and testing the mettle and rectitude of those who seek access into the fellowship of arms. The modern version of this ancient tradition can be found, in part, in our military academies for officers, and our recruit training centers, i.e. boot camps, for enlisted personnel.

The Quest—The Fellowship of Arms

This transformational process, though complex and multi-faceted, is basic discipleship in action.

Most adverse cultural influences are filtered out in this process. Indeed some of the finest warriors in history are now cultivated in these storied institutions, matured in a martial culture, and thus prepared to face, fight and subdue the fury of our enemies. The question then arises, "Could Christian leaders be more effective in preparing believers to face, fight and subdue the fury of spiritual darkness and the demonic forces arrayed against them?" This manual, *Born to be a Warrior*, is intended to quicken the warrior spirit and assist, equip and motivate Christians to face, fight, and subdue the fury of our spiritual enemy.

> SELF-DISCIPLINE BEGINS WITH A MASTERY OF YOUR THOUGHTS. IF YOU CAN'T CONTROL WHAT YOU THINK, YOU CAN'T CONTROL WHAT YOU DO.
>
> —NAPOLEON HILL

Part 1—Born To Be A Warrior

The warrior spirit is the passionate desire and determination in the heart of a man, a desire to perfect himself for the stance against evil in the service to others.

— Barney Barnes

Courage, above all things, is the first quality of a warrior.

— Baron Karl Von Clausewitz

Chapter 2

THE DREAM IN EVERY LITTLE BOY'S HEART

For of all sad words of tongue and pen, the saddest are these: "It might have been."
—John Greenleaf Whittier

Little boys seem naturally bent to face, fight and subdue the fury of imaginary enemies. They have a dream within them to do just that. Anyone who has witnessed boys at play will surely be aware of this fact. The cultural emphasis on political correctness does not appear to significantly alter this phenomenon. I was looking at some of my boyhood pictures recently, and there I was, Roy Rogers hat, vest, and leg chaps, and a genuine leather, Gene Autry Flying A Ranch double holster, with twin six shooter cap pistols. I remember wearing all this warrior paraphernalia to school in the 2nd grade. Some older readers may have had a similar experience.

My desk was at the end of the first row on the right as you came into the room. So while in class I would hang my holsters, inlaid with silver conchos, and my twin six

Part 1—Born To Be A Warrior

shooters over the back of my desk. My teacher, and all of my classmates as well, were very well protected. In today's culture I would have surely been expelled, and my parents severely reprimanded for such errant and irresponsible behavior. At age 65, I still have those double holsters, with my eye on them as a gift to a certain six year old grandson.

The dream in every little boy's heart... to be a warrior. This is yours truly, the little boy with Roy Rogers hat and Gene Autry Flying A Ranch holsters. The shadow you see is my Dad, Rev. "Shorty" Barnes, holding the big square box Kodak camera.

You may recall, in the seasonal classic *A Christmas Story*, Ralphie is consumed with the thought of getting a genuine Red Ryder BB gun. In an action packed day dream, his family is gripped with fear as his home is under

The Dream in Every Little Boy's Heart

siege by Black Bart and his evil gang of outlaws. The hero Ralphie, armed with his trusty BB gun, single-handedly defeats Black Bart and his entire gang, thus saving the family from certain plunder. I believe little boys have this warrior DNA coded into their maleness, to be used for good as they grow into men; to foil the plans of evil Black Bart and his cronies.

Like Ralphie, I really cherished the thought of a Red Ryder BB gun. However, like Ralphie's mom, my dear mother also feared that I would shoot somebody's eye out. That thought carried the day at our house. I would later graduate from cap pistols to a .22 caliber rifle that my Dad would train me to clean, handle, and shoot.

In those days, firearms safety and marksmanship were a standard home course for young boys in rural East Tennessee. We would go down to Arthur Fox's store and Dad, who was a Baptist pastor, would buy a box of fifty .22 caliber Remington "shorts" for fifty cents. Then we'd go just about a mile, to Granddaddy's farm for target practice. We always stepped off 20 paces from the target, which of course, was a tin can set about five feet high, on the side of the wood shed. Yes, there really was a wood shed. After mastering the challenge of shooting the can upright, the can was turned on its side, presenting a shiny three inch circle for a target. I still have that rifle, the many fond memories associated with it, and those great times I enjoyed with my Dad, my hero!

Part 1—Born To Be A Warrior

John Eldredge writes of his own experience of warrior dreams and BB guns as a young boy. In his classic for men, *Wild at Heart*, he writes about boyhood summers spent on his grandfather's working ranch in Oregon. He relates that on one occasion, his grandfather, known as Pop, took him to town to John's favorite store. This store was filled with supplies that a rancher would need, grain feed, hay, tack, hardware, and leather, along with all the distinctive smells and aromas. Eldredge writes, "Pop walked straight over to the firearms counter, picked out a BB rifle and a quart-sized milk carton, with about a million BBs in it, and handed them to me."

Eldredge relates that the storekeeper questioned Pop's judgment, thinking the boy was too young. Pop simply responded by putting his hand on young John's shoulder and said, "This is my grandson Hal. He's riding shotgun for me." Eldredge goes on to make this very profound observation. "I may have walked into that feed store a squirrelly little kid, but I walked out as Sheriff Wyatt Earp. I had an identity and a place in the story. I was invited to be dangerous. If a boy is to become a man, if a man is to know he is one, this is not an option. A man has to know where he comes from and what he is made of."

> "A MAN HAS TO KNOW WHERE HE COMES FROM AND WHAT HE IS MADE OF."
> —JOHN ELDREDGE

The Dream in Every Little Boy's Heart

The classic story of the legendary knight, Saint George, a man who surely knew what he was made of, is worth reviewing here. This tale of hero, heroine and villain is the timeless theme of the fantasies of little boys, and little girls as well. It is a perennial theme of many Hollywood and television movies. In this story Sir George, a kind and brave knight, is the embodiment of hero lore. As such, he eventually becomes St. George.

Dr. William J. Bennett relates this story in his wonderful little book *Virtues of Leadership*. One day, so the story goes, Sir George realizes that his domain has been pacified. There is no fear of crime or wild animals, children can safely play everywhere, even in the nearby forest. As he rode through the country side, our noble knight observed the industrious activity and domestic harmony of a safe and happy people, and thought to himself, "I am no longer needed here."

Work That Only a Knight Can Do

Sir George, from that hour began to ponder the thought, "Somewhere, perhaps there is trouble and fear. There may be some place where little children cannot play in safety, where perhaps a woman may have been carried away from her home, or perhaps where there are even dragons left to be slain. Tomorrow I shall ride away and never stop until I find work which only a knight can do." This thought perfectly captures a little boy's dreams.

Part 1—Born To Be A Warrior

As the story unfolds our fearless knight finds such a place and "the work that only a knight can do." He finds an empty village and burned out fields, a castle filled with desperately fearful people, and a fair maiden in distress. He discovers that one evil dragon has been the source of all the terror and fear. He quickly locates the dragon and, of course an epic battle between good and evil ensues. There is the ebb and flow of mortal combat—the giant fire breathing dragon vs. the brave and handsome knight. At the last moment, the hero delivers a fatal blow to the beast, the heroine is saved and they all live happily ever after. Such is the dream, or one quite similar, that most little boys have dreamt. Little girls, too!

Dr. Bennett describes our knight's motivation. "Here we see the course of a morally ambitious consciousness, habitually searching to aid others." One could argue that we are born amoral, but I believe this morally ambitious consciousness resides within us and is part of the DNA genetic code of the warrior spirit. Neither Ralphie, John Eldredge, nor I had to be re-educated to desire a Red Ryder BB gun. We just happened to be little boys.

My daughters remember well my telling them the story of Saint George. It was told them with a view to possibly explain some of my own behaviors and motivations, as well as what to look for in a husband. Often when we go visit them, I am greeted with "Hi Dad, I have some work that only a knight can do." Immediately, I know I am needed. A washing machine or a sink disposal has malfunctioned. Something on their vehicle is making a

The Dream in Every Little Boy's Heart

funny noise. Perhaps a grand child needs to be read a story or taken for a discovery adventure of some sort. All of a sudden I am on a glorious quest and no longer bored. I have found work that only a knight can do.

Looking for work... "that only a knight can do."

SOMEWHERE PERHAPS THERE IS TROUBLE AND FEAR... PERHAPS WHERE THERE ARE EVEN DRAGONS LEFT TO BE SLAIN. TOMORROW I SHALL RIDE AWAY AND NEVER STOP UNTIL I FIND WORK WHICH ONLY A KNIGHT CAN DO.

-SIR GEORGE
Saint George and the Dragon

Part 1—Born To Be A Warrior

> *... Not by might, nor by power, but by my Spirit says the Lord Almighty.*
> *Zechariah 4:6 (NIV)*

YOU KNOW, I AM SURE, THAT NOT NUMBERS OR STRENGTH BRING VICTORY IN WAR, BUT WHICHEVER ARMY GOES INTO BATTLE STRONGER IN SOUL, THEIR ENEMIES GENERALLY CANNOT WITHSTAND THEM.

-XENOPHON

Chapter 3

DEFINING THE WARRIOR CODE

The bars of life at which we fret,
That seem to prison and control,
Are but the doors of daring, set
Ajar before the soul.
Say not, "too poor, but freely give,"
Sigh not, "Too weak," but boldly try;
You never can begin to live
Until you dare to die.

—Henry Van Dyke
Doors of Daring

I heartily recommend that you read *The Faith of the American Soldier*, a very scholarly and inspiring book written in 2005 by Stephen Mansfield. In chapter four he writes about warrior codes. "The warrior code takes a soldier and makes him a knight. It connects the natural life of a fighter to the supernatural understanding of the warrior calling. His duties are transformed into holy sacrifices; his sense of self is reformed into an image of the servant in pursuit of valor. He becomes part of a

Part 1—Born To Be A Warrior

fellowship, a noble tradition that flows through him and carries him beyond the mediocre and the vain." This is warrior talk and speaks to the heart, not the head. It speaks of a life-style devoted to the service of others. Just imagine the dynamic shift in our culture if every Christian man held such a warrior code that he could identify with and live by. "Jesusesque" indeed!

During the nation's history, millions of men (and women) have taken a formal oath by which they swear "to uphold and defend the Constitution of the United States against all enemies, both foreign and domestic." I have taken such an oath twice, once in the military; again for law enforcement. During World War II over 16 million American men entered into the fellowship of arms taking the same oath. When our wars are over, or retirement is at hand, these same people have populated, enriched and led, at all levels of the public and private sector.

Today the nation has some 850 thousand police officers, and 2.2 million military personnel. However, we have almost three times the total population we had in 1941. Accordingly, the per capita pool of Americans who have lived by a warrior code in some form has shrunk dramatically. This fact does not set aside the need for a warrior code in our culture, and particularly among Christian men.

> THERE IS A NEED FOR A WARRIOR CODE IN OUR CULTURE.

Defining The Warrior Code

The familiar imagery of the "long gray line" for the soldier, and the "thin blue line" for law enforcement, speaks of the fellowship and noble tradition we have been discussing. As Mansfield writes, it is "a noble tradition that flows through him and carries him beyond the mediocre and the vain." Yet, the Christian warrior needs a spiritual warrior code, much like Mansfield makes the case for the natural warrior.

The writer of Hebrews reveals another line in chapter 12 in which he discusses in detail what I will call the "eternal red line." This line is a sacred fellowship, and is in fact, the noblest of traditions. The long gray line, like the thin blue line, have a grand and glorious, albeit, finite purpose. The eternal red line has greater grandeur and greater glory and has an eternal purpose. Christian men must have a pronounced sense of entering into this sacred fellowship and personal identity with this noble tradition. In this way a river of life can then flow through them, bringing life to the culture around them.

Too often our churches are more like our well meaning service organizations than an army of holy warriors, made alive by the blood of Christ. The divine purpose of such spiritual warriors is to quell the fury of satanic forces, and project the love of their Lord into the culture. Perhaps the following discussion will clarify this important point.

Part 1—Born To Be A Warrior

In ancient Sparta, the warrior's shield became a legendary part of their armor. The tradition was that Mothers presented their sons with their shield with this command: "Spartan, here is your shield. Come back bearing this shield or being borne upon it."

CHAPTER 4

THE SAMURAI, THE KNIGHT AND JESUS

THE SAMURAI

Entrance into the Samurai system began as a boy, combining years of physical training with years of studying Japanese history, culture, poetry, and spiritual discipline. The young candidates were immersed in extensive sword training, a primary focus of Kendo—the way of (*do*) the sword (*ken*). The candidate was simultaneously immersed in the moral code of the Samurai, as well as Zen Buddhism. The classic Hollywood film *Shogun* showcases this martial lifestyle and culture in a very accurate and graphic manner. Good movie!

This intense regimen was developed over centuries, to prepare a young man to live his life according to Bushido, the way of (*do*) the warrior (*bushi*). Bushido was an all encompassing life style that was expressed in seven virtues or character qualities: rectitude, courage, benevolence, respect, honesty, honor, and loyalty. The

Part 1—Born To Be A Warrior

etiquette of self-sacrifice was instilled from childhood through an often unuttered and unwritten instinctive code. Most pastors I have known would love to have a congregation full of such well behaved, dedicated, generous, upright, dependable and self-sacrificing men. Where are they?

In the history of warfare some precepts and principles are unchanging. One of those precepts is that the weapon is the extension of the warrior. In the case of the Samurai, it could be said that the warrior and his weapon were one, a marriage if you will. The Samurai warrior occupies a revered place of honor in the chronicles of warfare, and is always accompanied by his Samurai sword. The process of making the warrior was remarkably analogous with the process of making the weapon, both of which were carefully forged, tempered, and repeatedly purified by the fiery furnace, the hammer and the anvil.

> THE SAMURAI WARRIOR WAS ONE WITH HIS WEAPON.

True Samurai swords are made by hand and are still made today. They remain quite popular among martial artists. A Samurai sword could require months to fabricate, by a craftsman who trained for years to master the craft. In Japanese history, the making of a Samurai sword was viewed as a sacred calling.

The Samurai, The Knight and Jesus

The process begins with a bar of tamahagane, an extremely high quality steel that is melted, pounded, folded, flattened, and heated near white hot, over and over. When the metal is glowing white with heat, impurities can readily be seen and pounded out. The next process involves placing this purified steel into a sheath of higher carbon steel, known as *habe-gane*. This is followed by more heating, pounding and shaping. Thus, a unique weapon is created, one perfectly suited to the disposition of a Samurai warrior.

The Samurai warrior's character was the exact image of the Samurai sword. Both had been tempered in crucibles of heat and struggle, and the impurities had been identified and purged. Both were fabricated with strong laminates, carefully forged and molded into a unity of purpose. The Samurai warrior armed with a Samurai sword was a lethal weapon, slashing enemy swords into pieces and leaving enemy warriors defenseless and often in pieces.

The Knight

You will likely have greater familiarity with medieval knights, from literature or even from the movies. The legendary tales of King Arthur and the Knights of the Round Table are the epitome of the character in a medieval knight. We know that knights, like the fabled Sir Lancelot, served the king, fought valiantly against evil enemies, rescued fair maidens, and performed many other noble feats, all with the purist of motives. However,

Part 1—Born To Be A Warrior

the true purpose of these warriors extended far beyond the fabled Camelot.

The medieval knight emerged as a defender of the Church and all its related territory. That defense was the basis for the Crusades to the Holy Land to quell Muslim invaders. **A candidate for knighthood was required to prove that he could master himself before he could be trusted to master an enemy.** Moreover, the candidate was also obligated to prove himself to be under God's authority, before he was permitted to operate as a knight under the king's authority. As a knight, he no longer represented himself. Rather he represented his God and his king, in all of his actions, as well as his inactions. Again, most pastors I have known are looking for a few such men. Where are they?

The investiture of knighthood perfectly combined a candidate's holy passion and personal devotion to God with formidable might and martial skills. This transformational, discipleship process had been carefully crafted and perfected. Once a young squire became a knight, he fully accepted the requirements of his calling. Above all else he was required to maintain a pure heart and to live a holy life in the service of his God and his king.

> A KNIGHT WAS REQUIRED TO MAINTAIN A PURE HEART AND TO LIVE A HOLY LIFE IN THE SERVICE OF HIS GOD AND HIS KING.

The Samurai, The Knight and Jesus

In a final ceremony, a broad sword would be laid before the squire, one that had especially been crafted for his use in the service of God and king. A priest would invite other knights to join their hands to the "virgin" sword and pronounce a blessing much like this. "Bless this sword so that it may be a defense for Your Churches, for widows and orphans, and for Christians everywhere against the fury of the heathen."

And so the warrior spirit was awakened in the young knight in much the same way as it was in the young Samurai. The warrior spirit was then nurtured and tested in both systems until all the rites of passage were satisfied and completed. Then, and only then did a true warrior emerge. He was a man under authority, poised, prepared, armed and ready to engage any enemy threat, animated and sustained by the warrior spirit deep within.

Jesus, the Ultimate Warrior

The ultimate warrior and our consummate example is, Jesus Christ—the Lion of the Tribe of Judah. Completely submitted to his Father's will, he led a disciplined life of compassionate service and self-sacrifice. Our Native American brothers uniquely capture this essence when they refer to Jesus as "The Great Warrior Chief." That is a stand-alone superlative that I will not dilute with comment.

It was He who said to His Father "not my will, but yours." It was He who drew children to his side. It was He who cared for the needy. It was He who spent time with select men, making disciples. It was He who found time to pray, to discover, and then do Father's will. It was He who forcefully drove the money changers from "Papa's House." It was He who loved His mother, and it was He who walked miles and miles in service to others.

Finally, He came to a hill on the horizon. He had seen Golgotha looming ominously in the Spirit, long before the physical mount came into view. He pressed on undaunted. Our Lord Christ took this hill and planted himself, instead of a flag, victoriously atop Mount Calvary, on a cruel Roman cross. He endured that cross, despising its shame, and established a timeless symbol of victory, the Cross, a gift made available to us all.

Jesus faced and conquered death, the last enemy, and won the victory of life for all who would follow Him. In so doing, Jesus perfectly fulfilled our definition of warrior spirit: **a passionate desire and determination in the heart of a man, a desire to perfect himself for the stance against evil in the service to others.**

It was also Jesus who gave that great military command: "Follow Me." He did not say look at me, think about me or talk about me. The command, the challenge, the invitation was emphatically, "follow Me." This is warrior talk! Later, the apostle Paul exhorts those around him to follow him, or imitate him, as he follows Christ.

The Samurai, The Knight and Jesus

The word Paul uses is *mimeomai,* from which we derive the word mimic. The objective here is imitation, not admiration, and it comes in a continuous tense. *Mimeomai* also denotes a decisive act with permanent results. Jesus Christ is the Ultimate Warrior, the only one who can so transform the lives of those who follow him. He is the Great Warrior Chief, the King of Kings and Lord of Lords, and Our Great Warrior King.

> JESUS CHRIST IS THE ULTIMATE WARRIOR, THE ONLY ONE WHO CAN SO TRANSFORM THE LIVES OF THOSE WHO FOLLOW HIM.

And the things that you have heard from me from many witnesses, commit these to faithful men who will be able to teach others also.

2 Timothy 2:2 (NKJV)

Part 1—Born To Be A Warrior

IN THE HISTORY OF WARFARE SOME PRECEPTS AND PRINCIPLES ARE UNCHANGING. ONE OF THOSE PRECEPTS IS THAT THE WEAPON IS THE EXTENSION OF THE WARRIOR.

CHAPTER 5

DAVID AND THE WARRIOR SPIRIT

In general, we are familiar with the life of David, and most Christians would normally associate him with the term warrior spirit. I believe that when we study David as a shepherd boy we can gain some understanding about the nature of the warrior spirit residing in a young lad. This book title, *Born to be a Warrior, the Desire in Every Little Boy's Heart* describes young David well. This is the exciting story of a youngest son who, with steadfast determination and courage, was transformed from a shepherd boy into a slayer of evil giants, a conqueror of mighty armies, and finally became King of Israel.

The passages in 1 Samuel 16 and 17 chronicle the story. First, came Samuel's search for a new king to anoint the man God had chosen to replace Saul (a regime change of sorts). Secondly, Samuel discovered David tending sheep, only after examining his seven older brothers. Then, Samuel anointed David to become King of Israel. The narrative continues with David's call into Saul's service, his desire to silence the blasphemous Goliath, and ultimately

Part 1—Born To Be A Warrior

with David's victory over Goliath and the scattering of the Philistine Army.

When Samuel first came to Jesse to check out his sons, he initially looked on Eliab, the oldest, and said, *"Surely the Lord's anointed stands here"* (1 Samuel 16:6 NIV). However, in the next verse, God admonished Samuel not to look at physical stature alone, that while man may look to appearances, *"the Lord looks on the heart."* Much of the same basic criteria we discovered earlier regarding the requirements for Samurai warriors and medieval knights are encapsulated here. Simply put, the most foundational and fundamental part of the warrior spirit is a pure heart.

1. **THE WARRIOR SPIRIT IS ANIMATED BY YOUR CHARACTER, NOT ESTABLISHED BY YOUR RESUME.**

   David was selected for service to meet a need of the King based upon his character, conduct and general deportment rather than talent alone. He had been observed by one of the king's servants as *"a son of Jesse of Bethlehem, who knows how to play the harp. He is a brave man and a warrior. He speaks well…and the Lord is with him."* 1 Sam 16:18 NIV. The character qualities that had been developed in David were readily recognizable by others who were responsible for discerning such things.

2. **THE WARRIOR SPIRIT HAS A DESIRE, EVEN A PASSION TO SERVE.**

   David was a young man under authority who *"came to Saul and entered his service...and became one of his armor-bearers."* 1 Sam 16:21 NIV. David had learned the lessons of servanthood, obedience and chain of command well, all from just being a shepherd for his father, and the youngest of eight brothers.

3. **THE WARRIOR SPIRIT IS GOVERNED BY HUMILITY, IS ALERT AND DISCERNING OF SURROUNDING CONDITIONS, AND IS ALWAYS PREPARED TO RESPOND AS NECESSARY.**

   A warrior spirit had been allowed to form and be nourished within this humble and selfless shepherd boy. Because of this, a warrior could emerge in the camp of the king when confronted by his enemies. *Goliath...stepped out and shouted his usual defiance, and David heard it.* 1 Sam 17:23 NIV.

4. **THE WARRIOR SPIRIT NEVER REPRESENTS THE WARRIOR, BUT ALWAYS THE MASTER HE SERVES.**

   Even though David asked, *what would be done for the man who kills this Philistine?* 1 Samuel 17:26 NIV, his question was much more than a "what's in it for me?" In fact, this verse reveals the zeal and

Part 1—Born To Be A Warrior

passion that rose in the warrior spirit of David. When confronted by an enemy who was defying *"the armies of the living God,"* his righteous zeal leapt to the forefront. The essential principle it grasped is that David did not take this insult personally. The response David gave, he did so as the steadfast representative of the armies of the living God, not as a shepherd boy.

5. ## The warrior spirit is always confident but never arrogant.

    The very essence of David's understanding of himself was set on a collision course with all that Goliath represented. He was an Israelite of the tribe of Judah, a son of Jesse, a loyal servant of the king, and anointed of God by Samuel. And what was Goliath? He was an uncircumcised Philistine, a rude and demeaning champion of evil, and an enemy of the Israelites' God. Consequently, David could measure Goliath's true threat by only one standard—the magnitude of Jehovah God. An important part of David's preparation for his impending combat with Goliath is described in 1 Sam 17:34-36 NIV. His martial skills had been honed and perfected in combat. He faced and thwarted a viscous, hungry bear and an equally menacing lion who had carried off his father's sheep. David rescued the sheep by killing their captors by hand! His appeal to King Saul was that of an uncompromising, dedicated warrior. *"Your servant* killed both the lion and the bear; this uncircumcised Philistine shall be like one of them."

6. **THE WARRIOR SPIRIT CANNOT PROPERLY EXIST IN REBELLION AND WILL ONLY FUNCTION PROPERLY WHEN SUBMITTED TO ESTABLISHED AUTHORITY.**

David had learned to value loyalty and obedience and even though he had great confidence in the outcome of the battle with Goliath, he would not challenge Saul's authority to send him into battle. David however, was forthright and appropriately persuasive. Finally, King Saul relented and said, "*Go, and the Lord be with you.*" 1 Sam 17:37b NIV.

7. **THE WARRIOR SPIRIT DOES NOT ENGAGE IN RECKLESS ASSUMPTION, BUT METHODICALLY SEARCHES OUT ENEMY WEAKNESS TO EXPLOIT.**

David, like a young knight or a Samurai warrior, had been tested on numerous occasions and had developed his tactical skills. He knew that it would be foolhardy to utilize untested weapons in actual combat. The bear and the lion he had prevailed over were fast moving, agile and ferocious wild animals, especially when hungry. So he rejected the heavy armor of Saul in favor of his tested and proven weapons: a sling, five smooth stones, a pouch made of skin, and a staff. Though not mentioned in the text, I believe David saw Goliath as a large and slow moving target. I believe he may have even become familiar with Philistine armor. Perhaps he had looked carefully at his opponent's helmet in the distance as Goliath made his daily challenge.

8. THE WARRIOR SPIRIT IS NOT SWAYED BY EMOTION AND INSULTS BECAUSE THE WARRIOR IS FOCUSED ON OBEDIENCE TO THE WILL OF HIS MASTER.

The battle itself is very interesting, and I believe it instructive to consider what thoughts might have gone through this young warrior's mind. Perhaps the best indicators of his thinking would be what David and Goliath said to each other. Keep in mind that Goliath spoke first and arrogantly represented himself in all that he said. David then responded, not showing arrogance or braggadocio, or representing himself. Rather he confidently said *"I come against you in the name of the Lord Almighty, the God of the armies of Israel, whom you have defied."* (1 Samuel 17:45b NIV). Goliath's limited earthly vision could only focus on a small boy with a stick and some stones. David's spiritual vision saw past Goliath and focused on the Lord of Hosts.

9. **THE WARRIOR SPIRIT IS FOCUSED ON A TACTICAL IMPERATIVE, CONQUERING EVIL IN A MEASURED, DISCIPLINED, AND PRINCIPLED WAY. IT IS RESPONSIVE, NOT REACTIVE.**

    David had a strategy and employed tactics that were successful. Goliath had a strategy too, but employed tactics that were flawed. Perhaps Goliath's strategy included intimidation by words and physical size, impalement of David on his spear, or slicing up David with his sword. But he underestimated his opponent. David's strategy was to use his mobility, to control the rate of closure with the enemy, and to use the longer range and accuracy of his weapon on a pre-selected target. (See 1 Samuel 17:48-49 NIV). We do not know if Goliath got off a javelin throw or spear toss that David would have had to dodge. We do know that Goliath fell face down, probably with a resounding thud. To all appearances he was dead, and his sword still in the scabbard.

10. **THE WARRIOR SPIRIT IS CONQUEST-MINDED, BUT IS NOT SEEKING TO GAIN PERSONAL RECOGNITION.**

    The scripture states that David ran to Goliath and stood over him. Quite possibly David discovered what I believe he already suspected.

Part 1—Born To Be A Warrior

Goliath was still alive. David had no personal sword. So he drew Goliath's own sword cut off his head and killed him, just as he had prophesied he would do in 1 Samuel 17:46 NIV. Can you imagine how the Philistines must have reacted when David held up the head of Goliath? It is of paramount importance that we understand that this was the warrior spirit in operation, not a spirit of machismo or bravado. It is true that David had prophesied the outcome to Goliath. But the conclusion of verse 46 provides his motivation, *"and the whole world will know that there is a God in Israel."* He was not proclaiming to the earth that there was a David in Israel.

CHAPTER 6

THE WARRIOR SPIRIT IN MODERN CULTURE

> It is the unconquerable soul of man,
> not the nature of the weapons he uses,
> that insures victory.
> —General George Patton

Warrior is a term seldom used in our culture at large. Indeed, our culture is clearly uncomfortable using this terminology. In recent decades, the use of the term "warrior" had even become uncommon in much of regular military lexicon. Emphasis shifted away from the heroic leader archetype, so prominent in World War II. The emphasis gravitated increasingly toward manager and technologist types, which were heralded as the "Modern Army." There was a variety of reasons for this transition in language and spirit. However, unwittingly and unknowingly, the security of our nation was jeopardized in the process.

Operation Desert Storm proved to be a "sea change," a transformation in this kind of thinking. With the

Part 1—Born To Be A Warrior

emergence of General Norman Schwarzkopf as a heroic warrior leader, cast in the mold of General George Washington and General George S. Patton, things began to change. The warrior was once again distinguished as a vital contributor to national security, the general peace, and the defense of the American way.

Subsequent to this, the events of September 11, 2001 and the general emergence of The War on Terror, has precipitated a greater re-birth of the terms "warrior" and "warrior spirit," linked with "war fighter." Thankfully, these terms are in common usage again in all of the military services. General David Howell Petraeus, former Iraqi and Afghanistan commander, continues this heroic warrior leader tradition as the civilian Director of the Central Intelligence Agency.

> **The warrior spirit is integral to the effective operation and general conduct of spiritual warfare.**

There is a tremendous need in the Church today for just such a re-birth of the spiritual warrior. The warrior spirit is integral to the effective operation and general conduct of spiritual warfare. Our homes, our communities and our nation are crying out for the presence and protection afforded by the warrior spirit. Just as in the martial arena, these terms must have a place in the common, serious lexicon of the Church, as they did in the first century church.

Our homes, our communities and our cities cannot be won with managerial and technologist archetypes any more than these models can succeed in the 21st century urban battlefield with Jihadists or other terror mongers. The spiritual evil and the wickedness the Church faces today is formidable and determined. It manifests itself in many ways which affect every community, and to a very real degree, every home.

Paul often uses martial-type metaphors and imagery in his letters. *Wage the good warfare* (1 Timothy 1:18 NKJV), *endure hardship as a good soldier* (2 Timothy 2:3 NKJV), *the weapons of our warfare* (2 Corinthians 10:4 NKJV), *put on the whole armor of God* (Ephesians 6:11 NKJV), and *put on the armor of Light* (Romans 13:12 NKJV) provide an underlying perspective of the need for spiritual warriors. Apparently his message was intended for just that.

Knowing that the scriptures proclaim that the very purpose Jesus came was to destroy the works of the devil (See 1 John 3:8 NKJV) establishes some degree of a martial context for the Christian life. One could reasonably ask the question; **whatever happened to the concept of conquering evil?**

When we read of warfare in the Old Testament, and the exploits of the armies of Israel, the modern believer may not be able to relate at all. However, many of these

PART 1—BORN TO BE A WARRIOR

passages perfectly depict spiritual warfare. They give invaluable insight in the tactical and strategic arena. *"Blessed be the Lord my rock, Who teaches my hands to war and my fingers to fight"* is the cry of the warrior David in Psalm 144:1. It is just as relevant today as in the time of David, King of Israel. This will be discussed in some detail in the next section.

I challenge you to think seriously and pray sincerely about what you have just read. When contemplating the term warrior spirit now, what sort of mental picture do you get? Perhaps instead of a Samurai warrior you now picture Mother Teresa, or a first century Christian martyr instead of Saint George in shining armor. Perhaps you see a faithful intercessor or an inner city minister, rather than a Navy SEAL. Maybe you see a neighbor, a mentor, a school teacher, a fire fighter or other first responder. Hopefully you also see your pastor as well.

As for me, I see all of those mentioned and more. I also see my personal action hero, my Dad, who pastored Baptist churches in East Tennessee for over 60 years. He has joined that great cloud of witnesses, spoken of in Hebrews 12, and is now cheering me on.

After reviewing young David's life, and the various warrior types we discussed, I believe you have gleaned a better understanding of the warrior spirit as an essential part of your heritage. We will be discussing all this in much more detail throughout this manual. Our world is in desperate need of real heroes, not the icons of heroic

The Warrior Spirit in Modern Culture

acts portrayed in the movies and on television. We need men instilled with the warrior spirit who will embrace the warrior code, and live as warriors of the Cross.

Remember that, above all else, the key to unleashing the warrior spirit is in your heart. With that passionate desire in your heart to perfect yourself in the service to the King and to others, you too can become equipped to bring down a giant. Maybe you will slay a fierce dragon and rescue a fair maiden, or perhaps it will be you who rounds up Black Bart and his cronies and tosses them in the "clink."

Part 1—Born To Be A Warrior

A man must have a battle to fight, a great mission to his life that involves and yet transcends even home and family. He must have a cause to which he is devoted even unto death, for this is written into the fabric of his being. Listen carefully now: **you do.**

That is why God created you—to be his intimate **ally**, to join Him in the Great Battle. You have a specific place in the line, a mission God made for you.

—John Elderidge
Wild at Heart

PART ONE

BORN TO BE A WARRIOR

Thoughts for Individual Reflection or Group Discussion

Chapter 1

1. Have you ever considered yourself to be a warrior, spiritual or martial? Discuss.

2. How does a boy become a warrior? Discuss

3. What do you think prevented Cain from "manning up"?

Part 1—Born to Be a Warrior

Chapter 2

1. Try to remember your favorite "action hero" when you were a young boy. Discuss.

2. As a young boy, did you ever dream of rescuing someone from an evil force? Describe.

3. Discuss Sir George looking "for work that only a knight can do." Application today?

Chapter 3

1. How will a warrior code help you to be a more effective Christian?

2. Discuss the importance of membership in a noble tradition.

3. Reflect on the "long gray line," the "thin blue line" and the "eternal red line." Discuss.

Chapter 4

1. Can the Christian learn anything from the precepts of "Bushido?"

2. Discuss the relationship between warrior and weapon as it applies to a 21st century Christian

3. Discuss Jesus and the warrior spirit in operation. Discuss the 21st century application.

Thoughts for reflection or group discussion

Chapter 5

1. What was the major difference Samuel discerned between Eliab and David? Discuss.

2. What new warrior lessons have you learned from David's battle with Goliath?

3. Discuss differences between Goliath and David with regard to authority.

Chapter 6

1. Discuss the importance of the warrior spirit in all segments of our culture.

2. Identify a few people you know who have the warrior spirit. How is it manifested in them?

3. Discuss the key to unleashing the warrior spirit in our modern culture.

Part 1—Born to Be A Warrior

PART TWO

THE WARRIOR SPIRIT

PART 2—THE WARRIOR SPIRIT

THROUGHOUT HISTORY COMBAT HAS BEEN THE FINAL TEST ALONG THE ROUTE OF PASSAGE INTO THE FELLOWSHIP OF ARMS.

CHAPTER 7

THE ORIGIN OF THE WARRIOR SPIRIT DNA

Finally, my brethren, be strong in the Lord and in the power of His might. Put on the whole armor of God, that you may be able to stand against the wiles of the Devil.
Eph. 6:10-11 (NKJV)

The art of war teaches us to rely not on the likelihood of the enemy's not coming, but on our own readiness to receive him; not on the chance of his not attacking but rather on the fact that we have made our position unassailable.
Sun Tzu (544 BC-496 BC) <u>The Art of War</u>

The warrior spirit has been in our spiritual DNA from the beginning. Most Christians would be very familiar with the Genesis account declaring that man was "created in the image of God." He was then assigned the mission of

Part 2—The Warrior Spirit

subduing and ruling over all of God's creation, Genesis 1:27-28. Knowing that the cosmic war of good vs. evil would dominate the entire history of man, God most certainly created and equipped man, His image, to contend in this arena. I believe this divine equipping was, in part, the infusing of Adam with the warrior spirit.

Interestingly, Adam's initial confrontation with evil proved to be an epic debacle. The warrior spirit DNA, though dormant at that time, resided within him as part of his being created in God's image. The scriptures are replete with examples of the "sons of Adam" demonstrating, or failing to demonstrate, that the warrior spirit resided within them as their lives and their histories unfolded. The Great Hall of Faith, in Hebrews chapter 11 is a review of many of these descendants of Adam. They demonstrated the warrior spirit within them through their incredible exploits of faith and courage. *"…whose weakness was turned to strength, and who became powerful in battle and routed foreign armies"* (Heb. 11:34 NIV). Moses was one of those who, after years of preparation, finally completed his rites of passage. He would no longer act out of emotion representing himself. Rather his actions would now represent the God of Israel. God could now trust Moses to confront Pharaoh and lead the Israelites out of Egyptian captivity and through the Red Sea by whichever route God would choose.

Celebrating this epic victory, Moses and all Israel sang in triumph and praise to the Lord, as recorded in Exodus 15:1-18. Would not that have been an awesome moment

THE ORIGIN OF THE WARRIOR SPIRIT DNA

to have witnessed? Indeed as you read these words, it is a triumphant and somewhat graphic song of war. The important point I need to make here is that in verse 3 we see that the Lord is a *milchamah*, translated "warrior" or "man of war." In fact He is a victorious warrior because, *"Pharaoh's chariots and his army, He has hurled into the sea"* (Ex. 15:4 NKJV). Moses, with staff in one hand, must have given a fist pump here. Yeah!

The prophets, also mentioned in Hebrews 11, certainly include Jeremiah who had frequent encounters with evil. Jeremiah confirms Moses' affirmation of God's martial qualities. *"But the Lord is with me like a gibbor, (or geber) translated mighty, valiant man or warrior; "so my persecutors will stumble and not prevail"* (Jeremiah 20:11 NIV).

I believe we often miss an essential truth that God, along with having a father's heart also has a warrior's heart. David, the warrior king, was not at all confused about this. The familiar text of Psalm 24:8 NKJV states…*"Who is the King of Glory? The Lord strong and mighty, the Lord mighty in battle (gibbor)"* affirms this truth. It should resonate deep within our spirit and connect with and awaken the warrior spirit DNA placed there by God. In fact verses 7 and 9 speak to this awakening, *"Wake up, you sleepyhead*

> GOD, ALONG WITH HAVING A FATHER'S HEART, ALSO HAS A WARRIOR'S HEART.

Part 2—The warrior spirit

city! Wake up, you sleepyhead people! King-Glory is ready to enter" (The Message). This too should elicit a resounding "Yeah!"…with a fist pump.

> The courage of a soldier is heightened by his knowledge of his profession, and he only wants an opportunity to execute what he is convinced he has been perfectly taught. A handful of men, inured to war, proceed to certain victory, while on the contrary, numerous armies of undisciplined troops are but multitudes of men dragged to slaughter.
>
> —Flavius Vegetius
> 390 A.D., De Re Militari

CHAPTER 8

PIERCING THE SPIRITUAL DARKNESS WITH NIGHT FIGHTERS

I am laying more foundation for a discussion centered on the warrior spirit and our spiritual DNA. In so doing I will briefly mention two other warriors named in Hebrews 11, Abraham and Gideon. You may recall that in Genesis 14, Abram's nephew Lot, some relatives, and all their possessions were taken captive. One hostage who had been captured was able to escape and report the incident to Abram. Upon hearing this Abram "armed his 318 *chaniyk*— trained, initiated, practiced—servants who were born in his own house" (verse 14) to go in pursuit. It is always folly to expect untrained, uninitiated men to accomplish disciplined actions, as Vegetius reminds us in the above quote. **Discipleship training in the American Church has been declining for decades.** This trend has contributed to the declining influence of Christ in our culture.

Part 2—The warrior spirit

Based upon their orderly response, Abram had obviously prepared them for battle. Their successful pursuit covered about 90 miles, which speaks much of their mettle and ardor. Abram then divided his men, routed the enemy in a night attack, successfully freed all the hostages and recovered all his stuff. Such decisive action will cause any enemy to pause and think twice about messing with "your stuff." The Israeli raid on Entebbe, on July 4, 1976, reminds me of Abram's raid and is a modern example of the warrior spirit DNA in action in Abraham's natural seed. I recommend you review the incredible *Raid on Entebbe* online in conjunction with this study.

Having conducted some night attacks myself, I have always been intrigued by the tactical detail we are given in Judges 7 regarding the operation led by Gideon. This is especially true after learning about Gideon's own situational analysis or SA, "my clan is the weakest, and I am the least" (Jud. 6:15 NKJV). The warrior spirit resided within Gideon regardless of his physical size and emotional state. The angel of the Lord greeted Gideon, *"The Lord is with you gibbor or mighty warrior,* (man of fearless courage, Gideon 6:12, AMP). Remember, this is the same word used in referring to God in Ps. 24:8 and Jer. 20:11. **We really are created in Father's image!**

So Gideon and Purah carry out a pre-strike reconnaissance mission in 7:10, a great example of obedience, leadership and courage. The warrior spirit is coming alive in a small, weak body, previously governed by circumstance and fear. Gideon then returns to his band of warriors, orders them up, boldly prophesies victory, divides them into three companies, issues equipment, gives final orders to "watch me, follow my lead, do exactly what I do." What a great reality show this would have made. Then at midnight at the changing of the guard, (great timing) Gideon, leading one of the companies, personally launches the attack. Wow! We know the outcome.

Night attacks are very challenging, primarily because it is dark and you cannot see very well. Depth perception is shaky. Strange sounds are amplified as well. Some nights are clear, with a full moon, and are almost like day time. At sea, on the aircraft carrier we called those type of nights a "commander's moon." That's when the older aviators were on the flight schedule. Then there are the overcast, no moon nights that are like flying in an ink bottle. Regardless, my calling as a young natural warrior was to "own the night," the darker, the better. I like to think that Abram and Gideon were "no moon-type" night warriors.

Accordingly, spiritual warriors must be night fighters, just as Abram and Gideon were. Their victories were in natural darkness. Although evil is obviously very active

Part 2—The Warrior Spirit

after sundown, I am talking about spiritual darkness and the accompanying wickedness. We must not permit the enemy to own the night! To do so requires that *we fight at night*. Has kind of a ring, huh? We Fight At Night!

Chapter 9

OWNING THE NIGHT

These are the times which try men's souls. The summer soldier and the sunshine patriot, will in this crisis, shrink from the service of their country...Tyranny, like hell, is not easily conquered; yet we have this consolation with us, that the harder the conflict the more glorious the triumph. What we obtain too cheap, we esteem too lightly: It is dearness only which gives everything its value.

Thomas Paine December 17, 1776

The powerful words from Tom Paine's *The Crisis* describe the character, the will and the warrior spirit of those who would fight, and sometimes die for the cause of liberty. These few artful words defined those intrepid patriots who, with indomitable courage and stayed perseverance would march on, undaunted by miserable winter nights and sparse provisions.

Part 2—The warrior spirit

 Led and inspired by General George Washington, these are the heroic patriots whose mettle was severely tested crossing the ice laden Delaware River on that windy, cold, sleeting and snowy Christmas night of 1776. Who, after marching several miles through the night, launched a devastating surprise dawn attack on a superior, warm, and well-fed Hessian foe. The entire enemy force was killed or captured, with no American combat casualties. Two patriots did die from exposure to the weather.

 These are the same brave lads who marched, some 9000 strong, into the crucible of Valley Forge the following winter. It was in those severe and storied wintry conditions that they were trained and disciplined by Baron Von Steuben. By the spring of 1778 they had endured much and were reduced in numbers to just 6000. However, they had been molded into a formidable fighting force, a band of brothers. These were not mere summer soldiers or sunshine patriots, they were patriots infused with the warrior spirit. Men so resolute in mind, and passionate in heart to serve others, that they owned the night.

Chapter 10

MY PERSONAL PASSAGE INTO THE FELLOWSHIP OF ARMS

But the bravest are surely those that have the clearest vision of what is before them, glory and danger alike, and yet notwithstanding, go out and meet it.

Thucydides (460 BC-395 BC)

During my 24 year career as a naval officer and combat aviator I encountered many who were infused with a warrior spirit. I also knew some who were not. In fact I learned early on as a cadet, under the close tutelage of combat hardened Marine Corps Drill Instructors, that it was not the uniform that made the warrior.

The storied U.S. Marine Corps Drill Instructor has the primary mission to shape and mold, to push and pressure, to observe and evaluate each individual officer candidate, to determine suitability for leadership in the challenging and arduous arena of combat. In fact one critical area of

Part 2—The warrior spirit

grading was called Officer Like Qualities or simply OLQ. It is an indispensable and vital function these carefully chosen DIs continue to perform in 2011. Looking back on that time, January 1, 1969, those drill instructors were masters of the craft of shaping and molding useful vessels. They performed their craft well, carefully breaking and applying pressure to check for critical leaks. I remember some in my class only lasted a day or two.

My class, 01-69 began with around 75 young men who had just recently graduated from college. They had passed several aptitude, academic and psychological screenings, as well as a physical fitness evaluation. However, none of these tests could determine the presence of a warrior spirit. Accordingly, when the 56 remaining members of Class 01-69 were commissioned as naval officers 4 months later, most of them were fledgling aviators, and warriors. The intense rigors of another 16 months of flight training to earn the coveted "Wings of Gold" awaited us as yet another hurdle in the rite of passage. This hurdle would cause a few more of the 56 to stumble.

Finally and suddenly there comes the day of combat itself, that timeless crucible, when warrior meets warrior. Combat! The anxiety, the excitement, the sounds, the chaos, the emotion, the precision, the intensity, the totality, the violence, the finality…then comes the sudden, welcomed calm of a familiar "normal." Throughout history combat has been the final test along the route of passage into the fellowship of arms. A small number were tripped up by this last hurdle and were re-assigned.

Chapter 11

THE WORLD OF THE SEAWOLVES

"The soldier, above all other men, is required to practice the greatest act of religious training... sacrifice. In battle and in the face of danger and death, he discloses those divine attributes which his Maker gave when He created man in His own image. No physical courage and no brute instinct can take the place of Divine help which alone can sustain him."
General Douglas MacArthur

This is the very best way to love, put your life on the line for your friends.
— Jesus, (The Message.)

Forty-Four Navy Seawolves and Forty-Six Navy SEALs were killed in action in Vietnam. Their sacrifice demonstrated the highest standards of service set by Jesus and echoed by General MacArthur. A few of them I knew from training together and

Part 2—The warrior spirit

normal squadron life. All were young, all were brave, all were shipmates, all loved life, all were warriors and…all gave all.

My purpose in taking some time to briefly review some of my own personal journey in the fellowship of arms is to establish a measure of credibility, and provide a reference point for practical applications of the warrior spirit into the arena of spiritual warfare. As we briefly review the world of the Seawolves we will also look at some practical applications for Seawolf Principles in spiritual warfare. In a later chapter I will discuss the *Nine Principles of War*.

I am convinced that such a review will be very useful in the planning and execution of strategic and tactical spiritual warfare campaigns in the 21st Century. For Christians to prevail over such formidable, entrenched evil forces, we must move from a widespread, *anemic spiritual welfare* to a purposeful and dynamic *spiritual warfare*. To change from welfare to warfare is the quest.

> WE MUST MOVE FROM ANEMIC SPIRITUAL WELFARE TO DYNAMIC SPIRITUAL WARFARE.

The Seawolves were created for this war as part of the Navy Special Warfare Group that included SWIFT Boats and SEAL teams. As such, there was neither a previous unit history nor traditions to bring forward, except for the rich traditions of naval aviation. In hindsight, I believe this was a blessing, because we were free to use only tactics that had been tested and proven in this combat arena. This concept would certainly be useful in spiritual warfare planning that included launching into new arenas, sometimes called missions outreach.

The Seawolves had the high honor of being named by their enemy. *Voi Bien* in Vietnamese is translated Sea Wolf, and this name was used to design the squadron insignia. The mythical German wolf, "Lowenbrau" is depicted standing on his hind feet in an erect fighting stance. The fire breathing wolf is aggressively holding a trident with the right paw and a shield, depicting the ace of spades with the left. The trident represents the heritage of the sea, and the ace of spades is the card of death. The fire or flame represents the power to sustain.

The Seawolves represented their insignia well. They were numbered among the most feared, and were the most highly decorated Navy squadron of the Vietnam War. During the squadron's short life, Seawolf pilots and gunners were awarded five Navy Crosses, 31 Silver Stars, 219 Distinguished Flying Crosses, 156 Purple Hearts, 101 Bronze Stars, and numerous lesser awards and citations. Their innovative, skillful and aggressive actions kept the enemy off balance, while maintaining a kill ratio of over 100 to one.

Part 2—The Warrior Spirit

During the Vietnam War, South Vietnam was divided into four geographic areas by the Pentagon. The most northern area was I Corps, and the most southern was IV Corps or the Mekong Delta. It was here that the United States Navy had established a strong presence called the *brown water navy*. The delta was of strategic importance, being the home for vast, innumerable rice paddies, and was the "breadbasket" for the entire country, much

Our Area of Operation (AO). The Southeast Asia "Breadbasket." No roads, just a lot of canals, rice paddies and rivers. Intersection of waterways, with heavy foliage provided ideal ambush points.

like the American Midwest. Navy Special Warfare Group further divided the Mekong Delta area into nine regions, and placed two Seawolf gunships in nine remote staging bases called detachments. SEAL units, Swift Boats and Patrol Boats (PBRs) were often strategically co-located with Seawolves.

I was initially assigned to Detachment-6, along with a good friend with whom I had trained for twenty months. He also just happened to have been the best man at my wedding a few days before we left the United States. We "newbies" joined 8 other seasoned pilots and 8 door gunners, who comprised the wolf pack of Det-6, just as two of these veterans were about to end their tour. In the fire of daily air strikes that followed we newbies, out of necessity, were forged into this living band of brothers.

> "WAR DEVELOPS A SOUL IN A FIGHTING UNIT…"
> Gen. Geo. S. Patton

General George Patton once said, "War develops a soul in a fighting unit, and while there may not be many of the old men left, it takes very little yeast to leaven a lump of dough." The General must have been aware of 2 Timothy 2:2-3. In our case there was a lot of leaven, a lot of faithful men, and just us two new lumps of dough.

I learned early on of the concept, "area of operation or AO," and that I was to know it better than the back

Part 2—The Warrior Spirit

of my hand. The reason was that we Seawolves were responsible for responding swiftly and decisively to any enemy activity in our AO, be it day or night. Each gunship required 2 pilots and 2 door gunners. Tactical doctrine dictated that we always launch as a fire team of 2 gunships. (Sounds like Luke 10:1) Therefore, each mission required about half the detachment either to be on alert or in the air, and we usually were on duty for 24 hours, then we were off duty for the next 24 hour period.

Seawolf Crew. Two pilots and two door gunners and a lot of firepower.
Seawolves were given their name, *Voi Bien*, by our enemy.
The ancient wolf Lowenbrau is on the gunship nose.

When not on the flight schedule there were always other duties to tend to, such as reviewing intelligence reports, logistical matters, administrative support, physical fitness, reading letters from home and writing home, or building rapport with the locals. During my one year tour I flew 507 combat missions, some more memorable than others. My new normal was no longer the familiar calm and quiet I recognized after my first combat mission. My new normal was the austere, alive, violent, challenging, dangerous, thrilling, and very real brotherhood. Life became very simple, very alive, and very precious. Indeed, I longed to see and touch my wife and children.

I experienced all the excitement of a Samurai warrior, and all the adventure of a knight of the realm. A recently beleaguered outpost once dubbed us "the cavalry," and I thought "Yeah!" My sole purpose in life was to fly with warriors and assist the good guys while often ruining the day of the bad guys. It was like being John Wayne or King David every 24 hours. That, and maybe Zorro or the Lone Ranger, except there was no mask. Certainly no one had dreamed of coming to Vietnam, but as a little boy, most had experienced the dream, to come riding in, guns a-blazing, to save the day. For Seawolves, this was our defining purpose—one in which failure was not an option.

I believe such a life in spiritual martial matters is our calling and would be pleasing to our King. It would have excitement and adventure. It would be Jesusesque! We would no longer need to go to the movies to see artificial renditions of things we dream about doing. We would be the movie! Born to be a warrior—it was my dream as a young boy when I donned my Roy Rogers hat and Gene Autry double holster and pistols. It was my dream

PART 2—THE WARRIOR SPIRIT

throughout much of my career. And it is still my dream as a soldier of the Cross. My dream, as John Wayne might have said, is to die with my spiritual boots on, guns a-blazing.

Our AO was bordered by the Gulf of Thailand on the west, where I and my crew had to ditch one morning

The village of Song on Doc. Home of Seawolf Det 6 until overrun in September of 1970. All Seawolves escaped to fight another day.

due to an engine failure. The infamous triple-canopied U-Minh Forest (Forest of Darkness) was the north border, where a sizeable French force disappeared in the 1950s. Detachment-1's very active AO was on the south, and hundreds of square miles of canals, villages, and rice paddies was to the east. Our mission included daytime interdiction patrols, support of allied riverine units such as swift boats, allied fire support bases, Navy SEAL team operations, and neighboring Seawolf Detachments which sometimes needed some extra fire power.

The enemy was comprised of North Vietnamese Army (NVA) regulars, whose fathers had fought the Japanese and later the French for the same terrain, and various contingents of Viet Cong (VC) all of whom were generally well-trained and disciplined fighters. "Charlie," or "Chuck" as we referred to enemy combatants, would usually attack under the cover of darkness in a clandestine and insurgent manner. This might include a mortar or rocket attack on our base or some other allied base, followed by a ground attack, or probe of our perimeter.

A more subtle terrorist type of attack would be a homicide bomber, with satchel charges strapped to their body, attempting to breach our perimeter, kill off duty personnel, and perhaps create a diversion for another attacking element. Therefore *whoever owned the night* would prevail each night, control whatever territory was in question and in general, live a longer and fuller life. I do not recall any of our tactical doctrine that was based upon a concept of "owning the day." However, the enemy was normally not foolish enough to expose their position in daytime. Remember, our spiritual enemy operates in much the same manner.

Part 2—The Warrior Spirit

"Vietnamization," included training counterparts such as Lt. Trang.

Chapter 12

SEAWOLF PRINCIPLES OF WARFARE

Good tactics can save even the worst strategy. Bad tactics will destroy even the best strategy.

General George S. Patton (1885-1945)

"When torrential waters tosses boulders it is because of momentum. When the strike of a hawk breaks the body of its prey, it is because of timing."

Sun Tzu (544 BC-496 BC) <u>The Art of War</u>

BAPTISM BY FIRE

The very first fire fight involving Seawolves was on October 31, 1966, when two Navy PBRs (Patrol Boat River) encountered a superior force of 80 enemy boats (sampans and junks), transferring a Viet Cong battalion from one side of the Nam Thon River to another. After encountering fierce enemy fire from both sides of the river, as well as from some of the enemy river craft, the Navy PBRs made a tactical retreat while requesting a new asset,

Part 2—The Warrior Spirit

Navy air support. The newly commissioned Seawolves were scrambled, arriving overhead in 15 minutes.

Dusk was fast approaching as the PBRs and Seawolves began a very bold and intensive attack on this much larger enemy force. The battle lasted into the night for about 3 hours, until there was no return fire from the enemy who had scattered into the surrounding dense cover. The results of this initial Seawolf battle were astonishing. Over 60 enemy junks and sampans had been sunk by the PBR/Seawolf team, and six had been captured. The navy force suffered no fatalities, although a few PBR crewmen were wounded, while the enemy suffered very heavy losses. One of those wounded PBR crewmen was Petty Officer First Class James E. Williams.

Congressional Medal of Honor

The Congressional Medal of Honor was awarded to Petty Officer First Class James Elliot Williams for his heroic leadership and courage displayed during this intense battle of October 31, 1966. James E. Williams, who had also led coastal raiding parties in the Korean War, was *the most decorated enlisted man in the history of the United States Navy.* If you would like to become more familiar with this great warrior, just enter his name and "Medal of Honor" into your computer search engine. You can also read his citation at the official Congressional Medal of Honor web site www.cmohs.org. In a later chapter on honor I discuss this subject in some detail.

Seawolf Principles of Warfare

1. DECENTRALIZED AUTHORITY

Helicopter Attack (Light) Squadron Three, or HA (L)-3 was the formal name of the Seawolves whose headquarters was located in Binh Thuy, near the center of the Mekong Delta. Binh Thuy was in a pacified area and contained a large Air Force base, a Navy base and served as a main support base for many combat units operating in IV Corps. All major Seawolf helicopter and armament maintenance, as well as personnel, medical, and pay functions were conducted and controlled there.

*Our Joint Forces Command Bunker.
Landscaping was obviously not in the budget.*

Although a true symbiotic relationship existed between HQ and the nine detachments, the war really happened in the many battles and fire fights that occurred daily, *out there* in the detachment AO. You could spend an entire tour in Binh Thuy without being shot at, not so in the AO.

Part 2—The Warrior Spirit

This could be said of many headquarters throughout the history of warfare. They are intended to be a safe, or a "green" zone. This analogy is also true of many American churches. A relatively safe or "green" zone does exist inside the church building. However, there may be chaos, confusion, and danger (especially for children) in the surrounding communities. The inability to influence and change what goes on in the spiritual darkness of our communities and cities results in the violence on our streets, in our schools, as well as a growing problem of domestic violence. We must get out of our buildings.

2. STRATEGICALLY LOCATED/ TACTICALLY POISED

Instead of being confined within the walls of fortified cities, which the Romans considered as the refuge of weakness or pusillanimity, the legions were encamped on the banks of the great rivers, and along the frontiers of the barbarians"
E. Gibbon, The Decline and Fall of the Roman Empire

In war the proper location of strategic resources is critical, so that tactical operations can be the most effective. Seawolf detachments were tactical units, often located with Navy SEALs and armed patrol boats, near existing villages or along rivers or canals that were the main arteries of commerce. Tactically poised, our mission was to be a quick reaction strike force, essentially responding to friendly forces in contact with enemy forces. It was essential to initiate actions that would prevent the enemy from influencing the political or economic activity in our AO.

Locating units in this manner was very similar to the strategy of Roman Legions, which always encamped along great rivers and roads that were the main arteries of commerce. Seawolves, as well as Roman Legions knew that our tactical effectiveness would be neutralized by seeking the safety and comforts provided by "walls" such as Binh Thuy. Pusillanimous, mentioned in the above quote, is a word you may not be familiar with. However, it is a very important word in making this essential point about walls and buildings. The definition is graphic and telling—"*devoid of manly vigor; lacking courage and resolution; or marked by contemptible timidity; cowardly.*" Webster's 1828 Dictionary. Our modern parlance has shortened pusillanimous to "wus."

Accordingly, the Church must have a presence in the market place rather than simply marginalized into regular meetings in buildings with walls. The Church must be bold and present along the great streams and rivers of life and culture. In this we have two great models to look to. (1) Jesus, our consummate example,

> THE CHURCH MUST HAVE A PRESENCE IN THE MARKETPLACE.

was at home in the market place, in their towns and villages, finding and meeting needs, and making disciples in the marketplace of life. See Matthew 9:35. Jesus was certainly no "wus." (2) The first century Church began to change entire cultures by meeting from house to house, gaining a presence and influence in the community of life, and all without church buildings. They seem to have had much the same attitude about walls as the Roman Legions. The Church being strategically located and tactically employed rendered believers vulnerable to persecution, but effective in influencing the culture. Jesus did say…Go!

3. WARRIOR SPIRIT.

An army of sheep led by a lion is to be more feared than an army of lions led by a sheep.
Chabrias (415 BC-357 BC)

Chabrias was a celebrated Athenian mercenary general who served many kings and led various Greek armies to decisive victories beginning in 388 B.C. I came across his quote many years ago and of course it rings very true in the spirit of a warrior. We come into leadership situations such as this in every segment of our culture. **As a lion, it is very demoralizing to be following a sheep.**

Over time I have developed a corollary to Chabrais' brilliant maxim, *"An army of lions led by a lion is to be greatly feared by the enemies of sheep everywhere."*

Seawolf principles of warfare

Seawolves were never known to possess many sheep like qualities. During the day we were on the prowl. Most of the time we were just honing our skills, training and looking for opportunities to prevent adverse events, such as surprise night attacks from happening.

At night, many of our flights were known as "scrambles." That meant you ceased your card game, grabbed your gear and ran to your helicopter where the switches were preset for immediate start, just like in the

"Seawolf Gunships ready for launch. Rows of barrels provide some protection against mortar attacks. Note the open nature of the base beside the river and the exposed buildings. Definitely "non-pusillanimous."

Part 2—The warrior spirit

movies. Normally both gunships would be airborne and ready to proceed to suppress whatever enemy action had occurred in less than three minutes. It was imperative to clearly demonstrate to the attacking enemy unit that it was the Seawolves who actually owned that particular night. It would have been foolish to rest in the glory of past victories. Against a relentless and determined enemy, one can never be unguarded.

Throughout the history of war, great generals as well as military historians have clearly chronicled the paramount importance of the warrior spirit in determining who prevails on the battlefield. It seems to me that the early Church was filled with believers who possessed such a warrior spirit. *Fox's Book of Martyrs*, which should be required reading, graphically chronicles the indomitable courage and passion of these early Christians.

As I read of these numerous heroic acts of faith, courage and sacrifice I realized that many of these Christians could surely have earned our nation's highest military award, the Medal of Honor. They, of course, earned a much higher honor. What actually happened as a consequence of all the persecution was a rapidly spreading influence of Christianity. The indomitable courage of these heroes, in due course, transformed a pagan Roman authority and Greek culture into a Christian one. These were true soldiers of the Cross who were infused with the warrior spirit, who walked through the valley of death without fear, and who clearly were night fighters. Many carry this torch today in distant lands.

Seawolf principles of warfare

4. AVAILABILITY, RELIABILITY, AND TRUST

Whatever service your business or enterprise is established to provide, you must prove your availability as well as your reliability in order to establish a trust-based relationship. If you do not provide a sufficient level of service to earn the trust of your customers you will soon be out of business. Unfortunately this sometimes happens in typical American church life.

Navy Seawolf units were not exempt from this precept in their charge to provide security and protection to allied outposts and Vietnamese villages, riverine patrols and convoys, as well as providing fire power in support of Navy SEAL and swift boat operations. During the day we would sometimes fly out to various friendly positions, land and talk about tactics and various scenarios, as well as share thoughts of family and home. It was important that the people in our AO knew exactly what to expect of Seawolves, and for there to be a relationship of trust maintained between both parties. I suppose one could say that Seawolves had a bit of a pastoral slant.

> IF YOU DO NOT PROVIDE A SUFFICIENT LEVEL OF SERVICE TO EARN THE TRUST OF YOUR CUSTOMERS YOU WILL SOON BE OUT OF BUSINESS.

Part 2—The Warrior Spirit

I cannot over emphasize how important it was to let units in our AO know that no matter how ferocious the attack, or when the attack came, that if they called for assistance, Seawolves would respond. In this process we came to realize that we Seawolves were the only air combat unit that provided this level of service. Of course the attacks would come, and then we had the opportunity to demonstrate our reliability in restoring order to chaotic and dangerous situations. From these dynamic situations, strong and vibrant trust relationships were forged that are still alive today, over 40 years later. **Each community in America needs such a church.**

Today, an increasing number of families, and an entire generation of young people in particular, are looking for a spiritual Seawolf type of entity. They are looking for a relational strength or force that is available to them, a reliable source of help to call upon, and with whom they can build a trust-based relationship. There is an urgent need for the Church to have the *tactical imperative* and acumen to effectively deploy these types of resources.

From such a posture as this, vital trust-based relationships can be forged within local congregations (bands of brothers), then with schools, with communities, and with other local pastors and churches having a common vision. To have such a vibrant and alive church will put the enemy on notice and restore and build individual lives as well as communities, cities and even nations. See Luke 19:13-17.

> All that is necessary for evil to triumph is for good men to do nothing.
> Edmund Burke

> All that is necessary for good to triumph is for good men to do something.
> John R. "Barney" Barnes

5. STRIKE FEAR IN THE HEART OF THE ENEMY

> For God has not given us a spirit of fear, but of power and of love and of a sound mind.
> 2 Timothy 1:7 (NKJV)

The principle of striking fear in the heart of the enemy is critical to war and transcends the historical and cultural context. I believe that Paul, in the above text, was warning Christians to not fall victim to this truth.

As mentioned earlier, our enemy actually gave the Seawolves our name, *Voi Bien*. This was undoubtedly related to our propensity to operate at night, but also because of our superior tactics and unique firepower. This included door mounted .50 cal and 7.62 mm mini guns in addition to the normal armament of forward firing 2.75 in rockets (10 and 17 pound), and twin mini guns, all accurately and violently delivered. The Navy SEAL teams, who were our "mates" and brothers were also a great nightmare for the enemy, and were know as "The Devils

Part 2—The Warrior Spirit

in Green Faces," and lesser know as "Devils Who Came From the Water."

Patrol Boat (PBR) torching a "Hootch" (enemy structure). Note the .50 Caliber turret adjacent to the "fire arrow." Earlier in the chapter, we discuss a fierce battle which results in Petty Officer James E. Williams being awarded the Congressional Medal of Honor. This is the type of boat in which he fought with Seawolf cover.

I do not ever recall the enemy, who was a deadly and formidable foe, as striking fear in my heart. That does not imply that I did not hunker down during mortar attacks. Looking back, I think that any fearless factor presence was because I was part of such a band of brothers who loved each other. It really is not much of a stretch to see the spiritual application today. Fear not! Even though your path takes you through the valley of the shadow of death, fear no evil. Not because of who you are, but because of whose you are. God is with you. Isaiah 52:12 declares that God goes before you and is your rear guard.

Seawolf Principles of Warfare

In martial terms we would say God has my 12 o'clock and my 6 o'clock.

Over the last several decades, many congregations have incorporated the concept of small groups or cell groups, much like the Church in the Book of Acts, meeting house to house. Within many of our churches are long established men's groups. Each of these has the potential to be a band of brothers. Some actually are. Such a band will be known for their passion to be like Christ, for their love for one another, and commitment to their pastor's vision. Such groups as these will mature as Christian warriors and, like Seawolves, will strike fear in the heart of the enemy.

> The Spartans do not inquire how many the enemy are, but where they are.
>
> —Agis II King of Sparta
> (427 BC-400 BC)

Part 2—The Warrior Spirit

Even though your path takes you through the valley of the shadow of death—fear no evil.

Chapter 13

GETTING OUT OF BINH THUY

Too Many Spiritual Warfare Seminars, Too Few Spiritual Warfare Campaigns

Properly trained, equipped, released and acting under the authority of the local church, our many ministry groups and outreaches can have increased effectiveness in the tactical spiritual arena. I believe Paul comments on this in the familiar Ephesians 4:10-17 and II Corinthians 10:4-6 as well as other places. **I personally think Paul would have made a great Seawolf.** Prayer groups, men's ministry groups, small groups, women's groups, Bible studies, youth groups, all can have an effect similar to a Seawolf det on the local culture and the enemy's capacity to operate with impunity.

Part 2—The warrior spirit

Many Christians are regulars at weekly Bible studies, faithfully listen to great sermons, have read Ephesians 6:10-17 numerous times, own several Bibles, and may even know a few Greek and Hebrew words. However, all too often these same Christians, who have been trained and equipped for years, have yet to "get out of Binh Thuy", get assigned to a det and become a threat to the enemy.

Of course the entire church congregation could be, and many are, a non-pusillanimous, Seawolf det type of ministry. I am familiar with some of these congregations and they span the spectrum of denominational, non-denominational and inter-denominational flavors. Exactly how this phenomenon happens…that Jesus' commands are taken seriously and actually put into practice…I really do not know. That is not my purpose here. There are even congregations who support other congregations in joint operations against a common enemy. The analogy here would be like Seawolf Det-6 assisting Seawolf Det-8, or vice-versa, because they were of kindred spirit. Wow!

CHAPTER 14

FIRE FROM THE SKY

The Seawolves, in addition to being given their name, were also given the moniker "Fire From the Sky" by the enemy they faced. Consider the dynamic of a friendly forward fire base coming under a ferocious enemy attack at 1 am. Seawolves get the radio call to scramble for friendly forces in contact. Two heavily armed gunships launch within 3 minutes and proceed inbound for typically, a 5 to 30 minute flight. The Fire Team Leader (FTL) and wingman both pick up the radio calls from the "friendlies" and get a picture of how the attack is progressing, enemy strength, position, friendly casualties, etc.

As the fire team approaches, some things become obvious. The green tracer bullets are usually fired by enemy forces towards friendlies. Large flashes often indicate their mortar positions. The red tracers are usually friendly forces, and their origin can indicate if the fire base position has been held or not, and their destination can indicate the enemy's position. The spiritual warrior must often sort out these same issues,

Part 2—The warrior spirit

sometimes at 1 AM, to know how to direct the various spiritual weaponry available, (per 2 Cor. 10:4).

Upon arrival over the scene an accurate and devastating attack will commence as soon as the friendly position(s) and the enemy position(s) are verified, just like Abram, in Genesis 14:15 and Gideon, in Judges 7:17. The FTL would direct the particular tactics to be employed in this night strike. Much of our intercessory prayer and spiritual warfare campaigns are woefully lacking in planning, leadership, execution and adherence to tactical (scriptural) doctrine.

The following is a natural war attack that employs all four of these elements. If the FTL's call sign were "63" (my old call sign) and the wingman was "68" it would go something like this:

"68 this is 63."

"Go 63."

"Roger, I'm going to roll in 45 degrees to my right on my "3rd now" with rocket run and mini gun…expect a left break off target with half wagon wheel for .50 cal work. Cover my break. Put your rockets on my .50 rounds. Follow my break left, and saturate target with door mini gun. Then I'll assess. Copy that?"

"68, good copy."

This simulation indicates a good attack with predictable results, because of the order that constituted it. The FTL ordered an assessment before proceeding further. Not a bad idea for the spiritual warrior on occasion. Sometimes we make prayer and spiritual warfare so nebulous and vague in planning, leadership, execution and adherence to scriptural doctrine that **any severe impact upon the demonic forces must be viewed as accidental.** It does not have to be that way.

Night attacks are very demanding of your concentration, and extremely unforgiving of even a slight error in judgment. For one thing, it is dark. Then, all of a sudden it gets very noisy as the side-mounted mini guns make a great roar, firing 4000 rounds per minute. These are programmed for three second bursts, that is 200 rounds, and a wall of lead that looks like the 4th of July, especially when it is accompanied with rocket motors burning as they leave your side rocket pods.

The door guns firing, high explosive rockets impacting ground targets, and secondary explosions all add to the early morning cacophony. At some point you realize the green tracers coming at you are not a good thing and momentarily a thought may occur "How did I get here" or even "these guys do not like me at all." At that point you seem to come even more alive, perhaps motivated by the proximity to death. It is just another test to see who owns that night, something one can never really ever forget.

Much the same dynamic is the reality of spiritual warfare, a test of who owns the night. Spiritual wickedness and darkness must be confidently challenged and contended with, in the night. Our prayer must be

Part 2—The Warrior Spirit

fervent and focused like our tactics manual teaches. We must light up the darkness with Truth, even as Elijah the "night fighter" did so well (note James 5:16b-18). We must improve our capability in developing seasoned spiritual warriors (note Matthew 28:18-20).

> *The Lord will march out like a champion, like a warrior (gibbor) he will stir up his zeal; with a shout he will raise the batlle cry, and will triumph over His enemies.*
>
> Isaiah 42:13 (NIV)

CHAPTER 15

WHO WILL OWN THE NIGHT?

Thus, what is of supreme importance in war is to attack the enemy's strategy.
Sun Tzu (544 BC- 496 BC) <u>The Art of War</u>

For we do not wrestle against flesh and blood, but against principalities, against powers, against the rulers of the darkness of this age...
Ephesians 6:12a (NKJV)

Just as the enemy of the Seawolves operated in the cover of darkness, so our spiritual enemy's timeless strategy is to operate in spiritual darkness, the shadows and darkness of lies, deception, fear and doubt. One very important thing has changed since Adam's debacle we mentioned at the beginning of Part II. The second Adam has come! I say again that I am captivated by the scripture verse that says, *"for this purpose the Son of God was manifested, that He might destroy the works of the Devil"* (1 John 3:8 NKJV).

Part 2—The Warrior Spirit

If we trust Sun Tzu's above counsel, and in matters of war we should, then we would concentrate on formulating our strategies and developing out tactics around projecting Truth. When Jesus went one on one with Satan in the wilderness, he followed the pattern advocated by Sun Tzu. Now I say that tongue-in-cheek to make the point once again, natural and spiritual warfare are virtually seamless in principle. Jesus attacked Satan's strategy of lies, deception and twisting of Scripture by simply quoting the Word back to Satan. Remember, the weapon and the warrior are one—the weapon is an extension of the warrior. I cover this exchange extensively as a spiritual martial arts bout in a later chapter entitled *Center of Gravity*.

> NATURAL AND SPIRITUAL WARFARE ARE VIRTUALLY SEAMLESS IN PRINCIPLE.

This example set by our Lord should cause us to question our own purpose, and our relationship to evil. A very reasonable question arises. Whatever happened to the concept of conquering evil? Perhaps there have been too many spiritual warfare seminars and too few spiritual warfare campaigns in the last 40 years. Effective prayer, the type spoken of in Acts 12:5-16, James 5:16-18 and Jeremiah 18:1-10, is key and must undergird all of our spiritual warfare.

WHO WILL OWN THE NIGHT?

We often speak of prayer warriors but seldom acknowledge, support, encourage and honor them appropriately. I believe this increases our vulnerabilities in two important ways. (1) We fail to maximize the weakening and disrupting initiatives of various demonic activities in our area. (2) We fail to maximize our ability to hear from God and ensure the presence of angelic powers to be present on our behalf. (See Acts 11:27-29 and 12:5-7).

Effective intercessory prayer, as well as individual prayer, is like a combination of explosive naval gunfire—a robust air strike, combined with a radar intercept anti-missile system. In short it has an offensive component that softens up enemy positions a bit, and a defensive component that detects and quenches Satan's "fiery darts." If we are to prevail over spiritual darkness, we must do more than give lip service to prayer.

In Binh Thuy, at Seawolf headquarters, a large sign was erected for all Seawolves to see. When I visited there once or twice a month I would be sure to pause and read it. On the sign were these words:

War is an ugly thing, but not the ugliest of things. The decayed and degraded state of moral and patriotic feeling which thinks that nothing is worth war is much worse. The person who has nothing for which he is willing to fight, nothing which is more important than his own personal safety, is a miserable creature and has no chance of being free, unless made and kept so by the exertions of men better than himself.

Part 2—The warrior spirit

At the time I did not recognize this as a quote of John Stewart Mill (1806-1873), the influential British economist. I did, however, recognize the words as truths that rang in my heart toward natural warfare. They still do today in spiritual warfare.

It is a pathetic and pitiful site to see someone who has nothing they are willing to fight for, a miserable creature indeed. This is the type of quote that should elicit high fives and fist pumps, maybe even a "Yeah!" What does it elicit in you?

I reiterate the importance of the warrior spirit in our DNA and the concept of owning the night. These, together with the application of our timeless Seawolf Principles will serve in the conquering of spiritual darkness. Let's review them briefly:

- ✦ Get out of your building but not out from under your pastor.
- ✦ Develop a tactical presence as part of a unified strategic plan in your church, community or city, with a band of brothers.
- ✦ Cultivate a Warrior Spirit. Be on the prowl. Have the heart of a spiritual Seawolf.
- ✦ Establish a reputation for availability and reliability. Build trust relationships.
- ✦ Have an attitude of striking fear in the heart of the enemy. Be Jesusesque! *"For the Spirit in you is*

far stronger than anything in the world" (1 John 4:4 The Message).

You must be mentally and spiritually prepared for battle, for that is the nature of war. You must vehemently resist, with all that is within you, any desire to be a mere summer soldier or a sunshine patriot of the Cross of Christ. Do not have an arrogant spirit, but rather have the utmost humility and confidence that the King, whom you represent, has a plan to deploy you, and to stand with you, the one He loves, and gave Himself for. Remember also that you are no longer free to represent yourself. In all that you say and do, or fail to say or do, you represent your King.

> YOU MUST BE MENTALLY AND PHYSICALLY PREPARED FOR BATTLE, FOR THAT IS THE NATURE OF WAR.

Like young David and "least" Gideon, and countless other warriors before you, God's plan is based upon the Truth of His Word. You are to be that real life action hero your wife, your children, your friends, associates and neighbors are looking for. During the challenges of cadet training, our drill instructor would sometimes in close proximity of the nose, yell "attitude check!"

PART 2—THE WARRIOR SPIRIT

I have found that 1 Corinthians 16:13-14 is a good place for spiritual warriors to go for course correction and a fearless attitude check.

> Praise be to the Lord my Rock
> who trains my hands for war and
> my fingers for milchamah (battle).
> Psalm 144:1 (NIV)

PART TWO

THE WARRIOR SPIRIT

Thoughts for Individual Reflection or Group Discussion

Chapter 7

1. Define the term "warrior spirit." Then discuss.

2. Discuss the significance of warrior being in our DNA at creation.

3. Milchamah and gibbor, what do these Hebrew words have to do with men today?

4. We know our God has a father's heart. Discuss the fact that our God is a warrior.

Part 2—The Warrior Spirit

Chapter 8

1. What tactics in Abram's raid and Gideon's plan could you employ in spiritual warfare?

2. How do we know Abram practiced discipleship? Discuss.

Chapter 9

1. Discuss what "owning the night" means to the spiritual warrior.

2. What are some current examples of spiritual "summer soldiers and sunshine patriots?"

Chapter 10

1. Discuss rites of passage and the role of discipleship for spiritual warriors.

2. When, if ever, does a squire become a 'knight' in our culture? Discuss.

Personal Reflection/Group Discussion

Chapter 11

1. What spiritual applications can be applied today from the world of the Seawolves?

2. Discuss why a spiritual band of brothers is a good idea. How is one formed?

3. Discuss the differences between anemic spiritual welfare and dynamic spiritual warfare.

Chapter 12

1. Discuss the fundamental differences between strategy and tactics.

2. Discuss the term "pusillanimous" in terms of the Roman Legion and of men today.

3. Discuss the relationship of availability and reliability to trust, both personal and corporate.

4. How does the spiritual warrior strike fear in the heart of the enemy?

Part 2—The Warrior Spirit

Chapter 13

1. Too many Spiritual Warfare Seminars—Too Few Spiritual Warfare Campaigns. Discuss this idea.

2. Discuss the concept of a Seawolf type of men's group. How would it operate?

Chapter 14

1. What should we consider before we launch into spiritual warfare or respond to a prayer request?

2. What practical lessons can the spiritual warrior glean from Abram's raid in Genesis 14?

Chapter 15

1. Sun Tzu said that it was imperative to attack the enemy's strategy. How do we do that?

2. Discuss the term "Jesusesque" and how it must apply today.

3. Discuss the relationship between Psalm 144:1 to 2 Corinthians 10:4 and their relevance today.

PART THREE

THE WARRIOR IN ACTION/ WARRIOR QUALITIES

Part 3—The Warrior in Action / Warrior Qualities

The principle of acting under authority is a moral principle, and though viewed as power, authority is not absolute, it is delegated power.

CHAPTER 16

THE PROPER EXERCISE OF AUTHORITY: IN TEMPORAL AND SPRITUAL REALMS

The debased conduct of a rogue warrior or a rogue police officer is often glorified in our culture. The rogue spiritual warrior is plagued by the same spirit to rebel against authority and to represent himself rather than his spiritual authority.

> **Exercise** can be either a noun or a verb. In the 1828 edition of Webster's dictionary, the verb form is defined: *to discharge, wield or exert as in influence or authority; setting in action; practicing.*
>
> **Authority** is defined as: *legal or rightful power; a right to command or to act; jurisdiction.*

Part 3—The Warrior in Action / Warrior Qualities

> *"Becoming proficient in the proper exercise of your authority, temporal or spiritual, is a function of the merging of the knowledge and understanding of your authority, with the regular and proper exercise of your authority. Christians who seek to operate out from under authority and/or who are ignorant of their own capacity to exercise their authority often become casualties on the temporal and spiritual battlefields of life."*
>
> John R. "Barney" Barnes, CDR USN (Ret.)

Today's headlines are replete with chaotic and sometimes tragic events that often carry a back story involving authority. For the family to be successful and have integrity, discrete parental authority functions must be properly exercised. Most sociologists agree with this. A widespread abandonment of basic parental responsibilities (e.g. to love, to instill values, to set boundaries and to have quality time,) has gripped our culture. It demonstrates a wholesale failure by parents to exercise parental authority properly. The many documented cases of child abuse and spousal abuse further demonstrate and dramatically underscores that failure.

Many of our vital cultural institutions are being destabilized and weakened as well. A major causal factor is this same failure by duly constituted authorities to

THE PROPER EXERCISE OF AUTHORITY

exercise their authority properly. These institutions include government, business, finance and the church. Such failures point to a weakening individual American character. Some institutional leaders have become both careless and arrogant. Others have become passive in assuming the relevant and essential responsibilities of authority within their respective jurisdictions.

The principle of acting under authority is a moral principle, and though viewed as power, authority is not absolute, it is delegated power. Depending on the realm or jurisdiction in which they operate, legal, constitutional, moral, spiritual and positional authority structures have been compromised.

The Dynamic of Authority

In the United States, we are unique. "We the people" are the power holders. We delegate our power to others. We entrust certain levels of authority to our elected representatives for limited purposes and defined periods of time. They govern within the bounds of federal and state constitutions and the laws and ordinances derived from them. But they must do so in a manner that represents the desires of "We the people."

Much of our current national dilemma has resulted from the improper exercise of this entrusted authority. "We the people" have reneged at holding elected representatives accountable, and "We the people" are the ultimate grantors of that authority. This seems to be changing. In a similar manner, the failure of executives to properly exercise their authority in business and financial institutions has produced dozens of financial catastrophes. Such failures in leadership have shaken these institutions and the confidence of millions of Americans, not only in the failed ones, but in similar ones as well.

Likewise, the improper exercise of spiritual authority has weakened the American Church. On one level there has been the well-chronicled, improper exercise of authority. Numerous Catholic Priests have been exposed for sexually abusing young boys, but not Catholic priests alone. The scandal crazed media has been exceptionally hard on this particular segment of the Church. On the same note, a relentless parade of ministry leaders have also fallen. Their immoral behavior and philandering conduct has devastated countless lives. The media has been no more merciful to them, either. In the process, the faith of many has been needlessly challenged or compromised.

> THE IMPROPER EXERCISE OF SPIRITUAL AUTHORITY HAS WEAKENED THE AMERICAN CHURCH

Numerous other examples of avaricious misconduct, illicit sexual behavior and the improper exercise of authority have produced a rash of scandals among

THE PROPER EXERCISE OF AUTHORITY

political leaders, some who are famously identified by the media as Christians.

On a higher level, a far more important factor affects the relative strength of the American Church. The improper exercise of spiritual authority by Christians in general and Christian leaders in particular. For our instruction or training (see 2 Timothy 3:16), numerous examples of the proper and improper exercise of temporal and spiritual authority are listed throughout the Bible. Familiar episodes in the lives of Abraham, Moses, David and others provide vivid illustrations of this problem.

Notice the account of Jesus and the Roman Centurion, in the texts of Matthew 8 and Luke 7. In a far different manner, it succinctly demonstrates the pattern and the absolute necessity for those in authority to properly exercise their authority. The Centurion understood the extent and the limitation of his jurisdiction, and the authority he carried.

Because the Centurion clearly understood the boundaries of his own temporal authority, he could exercise his authority with relative autonomy, as long as he acted under the authority of Rome. The Centurion also knew that the authority of Rome was like strong armor. It provided a shield that protected him, as long as he operated under that shield, the authority of Imperial Rome.

Part 3—The Warrior in Action / Warrior Qualities

Significant to our discussion is this fact. The Centurion recognized the spiritual authority wielded by Jesus. He also recognized that Jesus operated in a jurisdiction totally separate from Rome. Jesus was rather astonished that the Centurion had such a comprehensive understanding of the similarity of temporal to spiritual authority. To paraphrase Jesus' response, "Wow, this Gentile soldier really gets it!" In fact, Jesus said that *the Centurion set the standard* for totally understanding what He was all about.

Combat aviators and law enforcement officers also have significant temporal authority, including the use of lethal force. They are equipped with the fire power and the training to exercise that authority. However, the exercise of their authority must be in accordance with their oaths of office and their training. In the field, they must act in accordance with orders, policies, procedures, doctrines, statutes, and ultimately the Constitution they are sworn to uphold and defend. By this principle, they are men and women under authority and this authority is established by God. (See Romans 13.)

Understand then, the authority for the defense of the nation and protection of the community is established by God. In America, this authority is delegated by "We the people" through our Constitution, to all those who serve and wear the various uniforms of military service and law enforcement.

Authority or *exousia* (Gr.) appears over 70 times in the New Testament and I find it fascinating to read the context of each verse. As you review them, you will discover recurrent themes, such as the people affirming that Jesus spoke with authority, Jesus affirming that His authority came from God, Jesus demonstrating His authority, demonic forces yielding to His authority, religious leaders being upset and questioning Jesus' authority, the folks being greatly blessed by Jesus' exercise of His authority, and that Jesus' plan was to delegate His authority to all those who would take up their cross and follow Him.

From The Book of Acts onward various disciples of Jesus who had come under His authority were exercising that authority given them. This authority was carried forward and exercised by the first century Christians with incredible results. I believe a most appropriate term to describe these first century believers would be "Jesusesque."

Operating Under Spiritual Authority

Herein resides a major problem today. On the one hand most Christians do not possess the clear understanding of their spiritual authority, as did first century believers. Consequently, they have very limited experience in exercising their spiritual authority. The results of this are predictable and readily apparent.

On the other hand many Christians seem to desire to be in The Kingdom and enjoy its benefits while remaining comfortable with a vague, distant concept of being under the King's authority. In addition, any thought of self-sacrifice in the service to others is quite foreign to their sense of reality.

This is often linked to a tepid commitment to rather specific requirements of the Kingdom, for example, fellowship, spiritual growth, prayer, worship, tithing, and other disciplines. One cannot imagine the chaos or danger we would live with, if our military or law enforcement personnel held such a vague understanding of their authority, or a comparable failure to be submitted to the cardinal requirements of that authority.

Jesus made some very profound statements like, *"I am the way the truth and the life"* and *"You are my disciples if you do the things I command you to do."* Much the same is true in the natural realm where the centurion operated "as a man under authority" and really a model for how we all should operate.

For example, a deputy sheriff is more than a graduate of the appropriate service academy, more than one who wears a uniform, carries a badge and gun, and drives a fast car. He must operate under layers of protective authority. Specifically, deputies—and all law enforcement officials, operate in accordance with an oath, agency policies and procedures, local ordinances and directives, the law, the Constitution and ultimately "We the people."

Virtually all of the headlines reporting rogue cops or rouge soldiers are stories of men stepping out from

THE PROPER EXERCISE OF AUTHORITY

under the authority they were sworn to represent. They began to represent themselves, and totally prostitute the authority they had been given. Much the same can be said of rogue spiritual warriors who unfortunately find their way into congregations as their counterparts do in the natural realm. In both cases, they remove these layers of authority that are like the layers of Kevlar on a bullet resistance, ballistic vest.

> THEY BEGAN TO REPRESENT THEMSELVES, AND TOTALLY PROSTITUTE THE AUTHORITY THEY HAD BEEN GIVEN.

Instead of Kevlar, the spiritual warrior's layers of protection include spiritual leaders, for example pastors, elders, bishops, deacons, mentors, oaths, covenants, agreements and ultimately the Bible. When you step out from under this authority (1.) you can no longer properly exercise true spiritual authority, you are a rebel; and (2.) you are no longer protected by that authority, you are exposed to evil.

My life experiences as a naval officer, combat pilot and law enforcement official have shown me that graduating from military basic training, as well as the police academy, are somewhat comparable to becoming a Christian. In both cases one enters a new realm; a new life style that requires significant changes in attitude and behavior. At the same time that individual forms specific allegiances and relationships to the new authorities over their lives.

I have vivid memories, as a new cadet, of my Marine Corp DI announcing, in an "in your face" manner, "Lad you now belong to the United States Navy." Although that was over 42 years ago I still remember Sgt. Jon Godwin, and how he "cared" for me.

Over the next 16 months I continued on the course he set, operating under authority, first becoming a naval officer and then a naval aviator. Another six months of advanced training prepared me for actual combat. I was then prepared to begin to exercise my authority, an experience I had to grow into. Much like proper physical exercise, repetition in properly exercising authority produces very predictable results. This same principle applies in the spiritual realm.

> Repetition in properly exercising authority produces very predictable results.

In much the same manner, the police academy graduate will have acquired knowledge of the law and the Constitution. He will have some tactical skills but will have no experience in actually exercising his newly delegated authority. Therefore, as the new graduate returns to his home agency, he is partnered

THE PROPER EXERCISE OF AUTHORITY

with a field training officer (FTO). Under this tutelage he learns by doing, how to properly exercise the authority he carries under various conditions and situations.

FTO programs are in reality, discipleship programs which bring new officers up to a confidence level whereby they can properly exercise the authority represented by the badge they wear. A similar process is applied to the basic training of a military graduate. I think when Jesus gave the command to make disciples, He had something in mind not unlike the FTO program and basic training.

We often recognize Paul's relationship with Timothy as an ideal model. Interestingly, a review of many of these seventy references to authority, mentioned earlier, shows this very process in action. However, Jesus was the consummate FTO and DI, imparting to and transforming His cadets and His recruits into the spiritual wielders of authority, and the world changers we read about. Be "Jesusesque!"

In exile on the island of Elba, Napoleon was asked who he thought was the greatest military leader in history. I paraphrase, but he responded that it was Jesus Christ. He went on to lament that his armies had all been vanquished, but the armies of Jesus Christ were still on the march.

Jesus also set up the ultimate plan and mechanism to establish and sustain a trans-century and trans-generational conquering army. This is often referred to as the five-fold ministry, which provides the blueprint for recruiting, training, equipping, inspiring and leading a vibrant and unified multi-national campaign. (See Ephesians 4:11-16.)

Spiritual warriors must be aware that failure to come under the authority structure established by God hampers and prevents the proper exercise of their spiritual authority. Becoming proficient in properly exercising authority, temporal or spiritual, is a merging of knowledge and understanding with experiential application.

A "Jesusesque" discipleship program will transform anemic and sleepy groups of Christian men into holy warriors for God who can and will properly exercise their authority. This is an acquired and tactical skill that is necessary for the warrior's success on the temporal and spiritual battlefields of life. Remember the Roman Centurion…ponder that spiritual warriors!

CHAPTER 17

THE WARRIOR AND HIS SWORD

When I blow the trumpet, I and all who are with me, then you also blow the trumpets on every side of the whole camp, and say, "The sword of the Lord and of Gideon!"

Judges 7:18 (NKJV)

Sword—A Weapon of War and a Symbol of Authority

In this verse of Scripture we find Gideon briefing his 300 warriors. They are in the final stages of launching a bold, three-prong, middle-of-the-night attack on a large enemy encampment. In this divinely contrived military action, it is the authority of the "Lord's sword" that carries the day. Instead of the standard armament of sword and shield, Gideon and his warriors carry a torch in one hand and a trumpet in the other. Surely at least one corporal must have looked at these "weapons" in his hands and

Part 3—The Warrior in Action / Warrior Qualities

thought, How can I conquer these evil Midianites with a torch and a trumpet?"

Sometimes we underestimate God's plan, and His desire to keep us humble, the actual position of our greatest strength and success. As the 300 trumpets sounded on Gideon's signal, from three directions, verse 27 tells us that the Lord caused the swords of the men in the enemy camp to be turned on each other. Wow! Obedience does have its rewards. In this ancient battle, elements of both natural and spiritual warfare merged dramatically, much as they sometimes do today. Ponder that a moment.

Throughout most of the history of warfare, the sword, in its many distinctive forms, has been an integral part of the warrior's weaponry. Some of the more familiar types are the Roman and Spartan short sword, the Cossack and Celtic saber, the Arabian Scimitar, the English broadsword, and of course the Japanese Samurai sword.

As we discussed in chapter one, with proper training, the weapon becomes an extension of the warrior and the authority he represents. The sword is by far, the most universal example of this martial precept. This principle continues today with the armament carried by our armed forces and law enforcement personnel. It extends to the high

> THE WEAPON SYSTEM IS SIMPLY AN EXTENSION OF THE WARRIOR.

THE WARRIOR AND HIS SWORD

tech weaponry employed in the remote battle areas of Afghanistan with our ground troops, the cockpits of our combat aircraft, and lethal and non-lethal weapons of law enforcement personnel. When in proper relationship with the warrior, the weapon system is simply an extension of the warrior—of his hands, his eyes, his thoughts and the authority he represents.

Have you noticed that Hollywood seems to have a fascination with the sword? For example, in the movie version of *Lord of the Rings Trilogy,* the High Elven sword was a center piece. You may recall from the movie that the Elven sword was unique in Middle-earth and represented the highest art of bringing warrior and weapon into oneness. The widely spaced grip was developed by the Elves to give them maximum rotation when moving the sword through the whirling strike. This distinctive attacking style was the Elven trademark. It is reminiscent of the real life Samurai sword-and-warrior "weapons system" we discussed in some detail in chapter one. You may want to review that section as well as the chapter on *Exercise of Authority* as they are very much related to the subject of this chapter.

Christian men certainly know that "sword" is used in the New Testament as a metaphor which describes the Word (of God). Have you ever wondered why? For example Paul instructs us in Ephesians 6:11 to *put on the full armor of God* and he details these pieces of armor from head to toe. As a final instruction in verse 17 he says, *"And take... the sword of the Spirit, which is the Word of God"* (NKJV).

PART 3—THE WARRIOR IN ACTION / WARRIOR QUALITIES

I believe that the answer to my question "why?" is related to the sub-title of this chapter, and to the unique martial and civil position the sword commanded in that day. It was a weapon of war. It was also a symbol of authority. In the New Testament era, the Roman army projected the power and authority of Rome over the known world. The Roman sword was the point of enforcing that power, and the sword carried by a legion commander represented his delegated authority from the Roman government. If conquered in battle the legion commander's sword would become a highly prized trophy of the victorious "barbarian" commander.

WIELDING THE WEAPON OF WAR

And yet so sensible were the Romans of the imperfection of valour without skill and practice that, in their language, the name of an army was borrowed from the word which signified exercise. (Romanorum exercitus.)

The Decline and Fall of the Roman Empire by Edward Gibbon.

Wield: to govern, rule. To handle with skill; to exercise one's authority with... (Webster's 1828 Dictionary).

Throughout history the sword, as well as our modern weapons systems are married to the warrior to project the power and will of the authority who sent them. When

THE WARRIOR AND HIS SWORD

I was a Navy combat pilot in Vietnam, or aboard an aircraft carrier in the Mediterranean, or on a diplomatic mission in the Middle East, I was an element of the power projection role of the United States Navy, as authorized by our Constitution. When I served as a State Guard Battalion Commander, and as Chief Deputy Sheriff, my authority was limited to those realms, as prescribed by the South Carolina Constitution and the Code of Laws. Therefore any time I acted, or failed to act with lethal, or non-lethal force, it was imperative that I acted skillfully and within the limitations of my authority.

Paul expresses this essential purpose for the sword in civil life very clearly.

> Let every soul be subject to the governing authorities. For there is no authority except from God, and the authorities that exist are appointed by God. Therefore whoever resists the authority resists the ordinance of God, and those who resist will bring judgment on themselves. For rulers are not a terror to good works, but to evil. Do you want to be unafraid of the authority? Do what is good, and you will have praise from the same. For he is God's minister to you for good. But if you do evil, be afraid; for he does not bear the sword in vain; for he is God's minister, an avenger to execute wrath on him who practices evil.
>
> Romans 13:1-4 NKJV

Part 3—The Warrior in Action / Warrior Qualities

While I served as a Chief Deputy, Sheriff Ray Nash followed the tradition of President George Washington, of taking the oath of office on an open Bible. For our Sheriff's Office ceremony, the Bible was opened to Romans 13 and the Sheriff would read the above text. He would then expound a bit on the relevance of these verses to our duty as deputy sheriffs.

The Sheriff would always call our attention to the fact that in many other countries, their chief officers were called "ministers," which is another word for servant. Whereas in our country, we have a Secretary of Defense, many nations have a Minister of Defense. In fact he would make the point that their highest office was that of Prime Minister, or the number one servant.

From this text, among other things, we were instructed to commend those who do good, and to strike fear in the hearts of those who would do evil, for we *were not to bear the sword in vain*. Those taking the oath would then place their right upon the open Bible. Because of the solemnity of the ceremony, and reverence for the Word, the purpose and authority for *"the office upon which I am about to enter...so help me God,"* could not have been more clear.

While serving at the Sheriff's Office I met "another Paul" who was a guest tactical trainer. This was Paul Castle who had been trained in the British police, and in elite military systems. Among numerous special mission assignments, Paul had been a body guard for the Queen of England, and a driver

THE WARRIOR AND HIS SWORD

for the British Prime Minister. His company, Sabre Tactical Training, specializes in tactical training for both police and military units. Paul clearly had a passion to train officrers and to prepare them to survive violent encounters.

Under Paul's dynamic tutelage we became more "at one with" our weapons. For example, we became proficient at field striping and assembling a Glock handgun five times in succession, while blind-folded and doing sit-ups. In hindsight, this was a real confidence builder. First, you refresh your skill at field stripping while seated at a table. Then, you work on field stripping the weapon at the table while blind-folded. Next, you field strip the pistol while doing sit-ups. And finally, your do it all—field stripping and reassembling the weapon five times in succession, while blind-folded and doing sit-ups. You might call this exercise hand-gun discipleship. Ever heard of line upon line precept upon precept?

We were also introduced to a new "hand gun shooting-and-tactical-carry-technique" called center axis relock, or CAR. This procedure doubled the rate of fire for most of us. It also improved shooting accuracy. In spiritual warfare terms, this could be compared to intense Bible study/discipleship training all day for two weeks. Remember the Romans' awareness and disdain for "the imperfection of valour without skill and practice."

A lot of seasoned deputies had to swallow their pride in order to become much more "at one" with their weapon.

Part 3—The Warrior in Action / Warrior Qualities

> **We must not only be alert and vigilant, we must be trained and prepared to fight.**

There is an urgent need for a similar concurrence between men and the Word in many of our Christian circles. We must not only be alert and vigilant, we must be trained and prepared to fight. With the passing of time, some of those officers fell back (sound familiar?) into their more conventional, comfortable mode while others maintained that new tactical relationship with their weapons.

The application of this natural warrior training system to the spiritual warrior is virtually seamless in concept. The fact is that Jesus commanded His followers to "make disciples." It is quite rare that discipleship is a tactical imperative in churches and Christian men's groups. How about yours?

On a lighter note for you who can do sit-ups, try saying a few Scripture verses while you "bang out" a few, no blindfold required. You might even try it with pushups, or while walking the dog.

Looking back these two, Paul Castle and the Apostle Paul held a lot in common, only in different realms. They both were intensely passionate about saving lives, building men, defeating evil and having a plan to accomplish these critical goals. The Apostle Paul knew that in order to do this a price would have to be paid. He tells us in 1 Corinthians 9:25 that those who competed in the (Olympic) games went into strict training. In verse 27, he explains that he had to discipline his own body to make it do what it should lest he become disqualified in spiritual realms. Ponder that a moment! The writer of Hebrews (possibly Paul,) then gives us what amounts to an advanced warrior training curriculum in Chapter 12. Graduates of the "Chapter 12 Course" would be similar to graduates of one of Paul Castle's intense courses.

It seems to me that many Christian men just do not have an understanding of the functional relationship between themselves as spiritual warriors and the sword of the Spirit. Paul describes this relationship with the powerful imagery of a Roman soldier in Ephesians 6. I have discussed this concept with several men whom I would consider mature Christians. When in conversation, I describe the basic precept that the weapon is the extension of the warrior (the warrior and his weapon are "as one.") I usually get an affirming head nod. But, when we advance the conversation and talk about the spiritual warrior being "as one" with the Word, to be wielded skillfully by the Christian soldier with authority and power, I often get puzzled looks.

As I mentioned above, I do believe part of this deficiency is simply a lack of understanding of the very practical aspect of our "oneness" with Jesus Christ, The Word---the sword of the Spirit. This same blind spot of warrior/weapon relationship can hinder the effectiveness of the natural warrior in employing the weapon that he has been duly authorized to carry and use.

For a moment consider another familiar text, II Corinthians 10:4-5, that describes some of our spiritual weapon's characteristics. True, our weapons are not made by Colt, Glock or Winchester. However, they are mighty and powerful in God. They pull down and demolish strongholds. And, they bring down every high thing that tries to exalt itself against the knowledge of God. Finally, they bring thoughts captive to the obedience of Christ. To this some men would say, Wow!

Hebrews 4:12 provides additional characteristics of our weaponry. It clearly communicates that *the Word is powerful and alive,* that it is *sharper than any two edged sword,* that it is sharp enough to divide between our soulish nature and our spirit, and can even discern *between the thoughts and intents of the heart.* Knowing this is true, why would any Christian man indulge in pop psychology, or hang on to every word of a Dr. Phil? Think what could happen if millions of American Christian men were "as one" with Hebrews 4:12!

Wielding the Sword Under Authority

Be sober, be vigilant; because your adversary the devil walks about like a roaring lion, seeking whom he may devour.
1 Peter 5:8 (NKJV)

THE WARRIOR AND HIS SWORD

The main threat to Satan and his minions is Truth, as projected by the Word. We know that Satan has had the strategy from the beginning to deceive and twist the truth, as he did with Eve. In fact Jesus said he was *a liar and the Father of lies* in John 8:44. We also know that Paul detailed the warrior's armor inventory (God's armor) in Ephesians 6, but sometimes we misunderstand why this armor is necessary. Some Christian men may go for days, months or even years without putting on the whole armor of God!

It is important that we suit up properly. But we must know the purpose. Paul clearly states in Ephesians 6:11 that we armor up so that *we can stand against the wiles* (deceitful strategies) *of the devil*. This is why it is so essential to be a spiritual warrior "at one" with your sword, the Word, and to be *protected by the whole armor of God*. Then you can follow the wisdom of the great warrior Sun Tzu—attack the enemy's strategy. We attack Satan's strategy with the Sword of the Spirit! TRUTH!

However, we do not attack as rogue warriors, out from under authority. Remember we discussed at length in earlier chapters that being under authority was like having layers of Kevlar in a ballistic vest, making us bullet resistant. Being under the authority of the Word in the spirit realm is like being under the authority of our Constitution in the natural realm. It yields both power and protection!

Part 3—The Warrior in Action / Warrior Qualities

The clearest examples of this principle are found in Matthew 8:8-9 and Luke 7:7-8 (please read). In these passages, a Roman Centurion explains the principle of being under authority. The Centurion clearly understands the breadth of his authority and its limits. He knows how to wield it skillfully as an official of the Roman government. He also knows that he is protected in his actions, so long as they are in harmony with Rome. He also clearly understands that Jesus represents a vastly different authority realm. The Centurion, to the amazement of Jesus, also understands how the authority of that realm is exercised. These texts and Proverbs 18:21 are worthy of careful reflection from time to time.

Courage, Command, and the Use of the Sword

A favorite painting of mine is called *Washington at Monmouth* by Emanuel Leutze, who also painted *Washington Crossing the Delaware*. The painting depicts General George Washington arriving at the scene of battle with half of his army, 5000 men, in full retreat. Washington is mounted facing the advancing enemy with his sword drawn and held high over his head for all to see. This was a courageous action on General Washington's part, making him a prime target.

The retreating soldiers, on seeing their beloved leader with sword drawn and facing the enemy, are inspired to turn, face and engage their enemy again. These men were under authority, and acted in harmony with the higher authority represented by Washington's sword. Thus, the outcome of the battle was totally reversed in favor of the American warriors. In all the noise of the battlefield and the chaos of the moment, voice commands would not have been audible.

It is unlikely that General Washington drew blood with his sword that day. However, he clearly wielded it as a symbol of his authority. Having it drawn and held in that manner, he commanded the attention of all, and would readily have used it with lethal force if necessary. The chaotic retreat of Americans, ordered under the sword of the inept Major General Charles Lee, instantly became a unified "attack" under the authority of the sword of their beloved and trusted commander.

It seems to me that under "the authority of the Word" is how we are to advance in spiritual warfare. Too often we are trying to advance under the authority of our programs, our doctrines, our traditions, our fresh ideas, the latest Christian book, and sometimes, I am sad to say, the latest secular book.

> UNDER "THE AUTHORITY OF THE WORD" IS HOW WE ARE TO ADVANCE IN SPIRITUAL WARFARE.

In situations where there once had been an anointed plan of advancement and conquest, Christians are barely holding on or even losing ground in American culture.

Part 3—The Warrior in Action / Warrior Qualities

Losing ground is a nice way of saying "being conquered." However, the authority of God's Word is forever settled. It is up to us to boldly wield the Sword. We continue to be "Plan A." Taking that to heart, many spiritual battles can be turned, just as General Washington and Gideon demonstrated for us.

The critical battle of Monmouth was fought on June 28, 1778 and was the first test of a revitalized American army coming out of the crucible of the bitter Valley Forge winter. The loss of this battle would have placed the fledgling American cause in great jeopardy. Consider what might have happened had General Washington left his sword in the scabbard at this most critical moment in history. The certain defeat of his army could have resulted, and with that Washington's sword would have ultimately been surrendered to General Cornwallis. Critical moments happen, albeit less spectacular ones, in our personal lives. *The outcomes are determined by the position of our sword.*

> THE OUTCOMES ARE DETERMINED BY THE POSITION OF OUR SWORD.

Some Christian men have their swords cleaned, polished and safely sheathed in their scabbard. They are only drawn on rare occasions, in a somewhat awkward manner. Such men may look good as ceremonial guards or as participants in a parade. In actual combat, they are rather useless. Meanwhile, major spiritual battles are raging in their homes, their workplaces, and their churches. Too often they look to a Dr. Phil or one of his guests to bring resolution to their life conflicts.

For all practical purposes, such men are unskilled recruits on very dangerous battlefields. Paul frames the issue perfectly in 1 Corinthians 3:1-3. *I gave you milk, not solid food, for you were not yet ready for it.* (vs. 2, NIV). Hebrews 5:12 echoes the same sad message. *You need milk, not solid food.*

Many Christian men have never been taught how to wield their sword (the Word). They are often overwhelmed when they stumble onto spiritual battlefields. **They stand armed, but dazed and helpless, because they have never developed a set of spiritual combat skills.**

Accordingly, men must be trained and equipped for war under the authority of the Word, just as natural warriors are under the authority of the Constitution. Paul gives us the basic blueprint for the origin of our authority. He outlines our spiritual relational architecture, identifies the authorized offices, the authority structure, enemy composition and tactics, our specific goals and objectives, and interpersonal relationship standards. This is the gist of Ephesians chapter 4. There are other such comprehensive Word "websites," but this is a good one to check out periodically for a "spiritual warrior refresher course."

Part 3—The Warrior in Action / Warrior Qualities

It is essential that we improve our tactical proficiency in spiritual warfare matters. As in natural war it can lead to a longer and fuller life, as well as improve a warrior's ability to properly represent the King he serves. Like the Elven warriors in Middle-earth who had the highest art of bringing warrior and weapon into perfect unity, so the Christian warrior's standard must be the Word. Just as the widely spaced grip on the Elven sword gave those warriors maximum rotation with a whirling strike, so must the spiritual warrior be with wielding the Sword of Truth...with a whirling strike!

> All men dream: but not equally. Those who dream by night in the dusty recesses of their minds wake in the day to find that it was vanity; but the dreamers of the day are dangerous men, for they may act their dreams with open eyes, to make it possible.
>
> -T.E. Lawrence
> *Lawrence of Arabia*

Chapter 18

THE WARRIOR AND HIS INTEGRITY

May integrity and uprightness protect me...
David, King of Israel

About Integrity

Integrity is one of those intrinsic values that secure the highest order in the ideals of martial cultures. The personal integrity of warriors is a timeless standard that transcends both historical and cultural divides. Throughout history, military leaders and philosophers alike have known that personal integrity is essential to unit integrity and is in turn, essential to the life of a nation.

Integrity is a powerful and dynamic word. When spoken, it elicits an affirming response in a warrior's heart. He intuitively knows that this is a call to the essence of his existence. To better understand this strength, one must understand the meaning and relationship of three words; integrity, disintegrate and integrate.

These three words are all derived from the same root word *integer*; defined as whole. From high school mathematics you may recall that an integer is a whole number, as distinguished from a fraction. Webster's 1944 Collegiate Dictionary defines our three words as follows.

Integrity: State of being complete, unbroken; moral soundness.

Disintegrate: *To separate into fragments, to destroy the wholeness, unity or identity of;*

Integrate: *To form into a complete or perfect whole.*

History gives us an unforgettable lesson on the relationship of these three words and how they help determine the destiny of individuals and nations. We will review a bit of history from a familiar subject, the Roman Empire. In considering how Roman Legions dealt with issues of integrity, I believe we can glean some truths for application in the 21st Century.

The Roman Legion and Integrity

Although the prowess of a private soldier must often escape the notice of fame, his own behavior might sometimes confer glory or disgrace on the company, the legion, or even the army, to whose honors he was associated. On his first entrance into the service, an oath was administered to him with every circumstance of solemnity. He promised never to desert his standard, to submit his own will to the commands of his leaders, and to sacrifice his life for the safety of the emperor and the empire. The attachment of the Roman troops to their standards was inspired by the united influence of religion and honor. The golden eagle, which glittered in the front of the legion, was the object of their fondest devotion; nor was it esteemed less impious than it was ignominious, to abandon that sacred ensign in the hour of danger.

—Edward Gibbon
<u>The Decline and Fall of the Roman Empire</u>

The oaths we take, the vows we make and the contracts we enter into are essential instruments to monitor and measure our integrity. It should be noted that the oath of service was renewed annually by every Roman legionary

Part 3—The Warrior in Action / Warrior Qualities

on the first day of January. Periodically reviewing and renewing of our oaths and vows is a sure way to guard our loyalties and "plus up" our integrity.

During the time of Christ, Imperial Rome had a standing army of about 375,000 men, divided into 30 legions with about 12,500 men in each legion. The principle fighters consisted of 6105 infantry and 726 cavalry soldiers. Today we would refer to these as "the trigger pullers." The remaining troops were combat engineers and administrative support. We will center this discussion on the infantry and the individual legionary, upon whose integrity the strength of the legion depended.

Every morning, as is common in martial life, the entire legion would stand in formation for a personnel inspection. The 6105 infantry would be assembled in ten cohorts. The 1st cohort, a double cohort of 1110 men, always occupied the post of honor, and was charged with the primary protection of the Eagle Standard (Lat: *Aquila*,) the symbol of the legion's honor. Entry into the 1st cohort was based on proven courage and valor in battle, not upon a written resume. This ensured that the legion's standard was never in danger of capture.

The soldier entrusted with carrying the eagle was called the *Aquilifer*, one rank below that of Centurion. Occupying this elevated position of trust, he was also the soldier's treasurer, in charge of the pay chest. The remaining nine cohorts consisted of 555 men each, all divided into appropriate units, led by Tribunes and then Centurions who were customarily in charge of 80 to 100 men.

As the inspecting Centurion would face each individual legionary, the soldier would strike the armor breastplate over his heart with his right fist. The armor was thicker there in order to protect the heart from blows and strikes by the enemy. As the legionary struck the armor, he would shout **integritas!**— which in Latin means, wholeness and completeness. The soldier was affirming the oath he had taken, and that he was undivided in his loyalties. He was prepared to defend the golden eagle, the *aquila*, and all that it represented with his own life.

The inspecting officer would listen closely to the ring that well-kept armor would emit, and for the sincerity of the affirmation. If satisfied that the armor had the integrity to protect the soldier, and that the legionary had the integrity to fight, he would move on to the next man. The legionary and his armor were integrated into the complete, whole warrior.

> THE LEGIONARY AND HIS ARMOR WERE INTEGRATED INTO THE COMPLETE, WHOLE WARRIOR.

During the period of the twelve Caesars, the Praetorians or the Imperial Guard gained greater influence and political power. Ultimately, they were selected from what we would call "politically correct" soldiers. They were given the best of equipment. But, during inspections they no longer struck their breastplate or shouted *integritas*. Instead, they struck their breastplate and shouted "hail Caesar," signifying that their heart belonged to the imperial personage. Their affections were no longer centered on the legion eagle and the Roman code of ideals and values, as enshrined in the oath previously taken by the legion. As time passed, the rift between the Praetorian Guard and the legions intensified. However, the "armor of integrity" continued to serve the legions well into the third century A.D.

General Charles C. Krulak, former Commandant of the Marine Corps, was the epitome of a warrior general. In a January 27, 2000 speech delivered to a Joint Services Conference, entitled <u>Integrity</u>, he quoted a 4th century Roman general who had written, "When because of negligence and laziness, parade ground drills were abandoned, the customary armor began to feel heavy since the soldiers rarely, if ever, wore it. Therefore they asked the Emperor to set aside the breastplates and mail, and then the helmets. So our soldiers fought the Goths without any protection for the heart and head, and were often beaten by distant archers. Although there were many disasters, which led to the loss of great cities, no one tried to restore the armor to the infantry. They took their armor off, and when the armor came off, so too came their integrity."

THE WARRIOR AND HIS INTERGRITY

From this brief look at the legions of Rome we can see the dynamic relationship between these three operative words integrate, integrity and disintegrate and their impact on the life of the legion, as well as the empire. The legion was virtually invincible when the legionary's oath integrated religion, honor and the higher ideals of Rome into a warrior code for which he was willing to sacrifice and die.

This process of integration or "forming a whole" produced integrity in the legionary as well as the legion. **This internalized integrity guarded the spirit of the warrior against fractionalized loyalties.** In much the same way the materials that formed his armor were integrated into a whole, providing protection for his physical heart and vital organs.

As time progressed the culture began to disintegrate, to separate into fragments, lose its unity and its identity. Eventually this "disintegration" penetrated the legion itself. The formidable legions of Julius and Augustus Caesar that had once been characterized by integrity had become fractionalized and weakened by the moral decay of the culture from where the soldiers were recruited.

The Battle of Allia, 387 AD, was a major defeat for the legions, just 11 miles from Rome. Defeat became more the norm than an anomaly for the Roman legions. The Roman general's lament, quoted by General Krulak, says it all. "They took their armor off, and when the armor came off so too came their integrity." The legion that had once been virtually invincible, confidently declaring *"integritas"* disintegrated, and in losing its integrity, lost its once distinct identity as well.

Integrity as a Life Style

Keep and guard your heart with all vigilance and above all that you guard, for out of it flow the springs of life.
Proverbs 4:23 (Amplified)

Finally, be strong in the Lord and in his mighty power. Put on the full armor of God so that you can take your stand against the devil's schemes.
Ephesians 6:10-11 (NIV)

There are many forces in our culture contending for our affections—our integrity. One powerful force that contends for our masculinity and manhood, I call the "Phil Donohue factor." This often manifests itself in effeminate roles, where soft, unmanly characteristics are portrayed as reasonable or correct models of manhood. They are basically boys in adult bodies.

We must remember that Satan's M.O. is clear: to steal, kill, and destroy the very plan of God. Accordingly, biblical manhood is a prime objective, targeted by demonic forces. In the absence of the integrity of biblical manhood, key vessels designed to be filled with the

THE WARRIOR AND HIS INTERGRITY

warrior spirit are missing. Few are left to occupy, and to face the fury of the heathen.

As Christian men and warriors we need to be challenged to wear the armor of integrity. Like the Roman legionary we must be intentional about putting it on daily and being accountable to others in that integrity. Our quiet time in prayer, reading and meditating on the Word and seeking God's direction will facilitate and integrate these actions within our core and make us whole.

> WE NEED TO BE CHALLENGED TO WEAR THE ARMOR OF INTEGRITY.

The armor of integrity is weighty. Nevertheless, we must never set it aside for greater ease or comfort. The Christian warrior must take full measure of its weight, and find comfort in its protective qualities. We must not leave our hearts and souls exposed to the blows and strikes of the enemy by foolishly operating without the armor of integrity.

As Christian soldiers our standard is The Cross, and like the legion behind their golden eagle, we must be on the march behind The Cross, ensuring its advance and protection during our watch. (Please check out the chapter entitled *Onward Christian Soldiers*). You may recall that the *aquila*, the legion standard represented the honor

Part 3—The Warrior in Action / Warrior Qualities

of the legion, and was the object of the soldier's fondest affection and devotion. So must The Cross be to the Christian soldier! Just as the legion's integrity protected the legion's honor, so will the Christian warrior's integrity protect the honor of the Kingdom.

I believe that every Christian soldier is called to be an *aquilifer*, a bearer of the standard. It is the highest of honors to bear the standard of The Cross, a fact so many Christian men do not seem to recognize. Meditate on that a moment!

My Dad was a Baptist pastor for over 60 years. I remember that in referring to a man's character, he was fond of saying that "taking the path of least resistance would cause even a mighty river to be crooked, as well as a mighty man."

Probably influenced by my Dad, a few years ago I came up with a definition of character that went something like this: "Character is the mortar that holds together the building blocks of our individual lives, our families, our communities and our nation providing integrity to our culture and our way of life." My Dad would say "keeping us straight." Confucius weighed in on the subject like this. "The strength of the nation derives from the integrity of the home."

A brick wall is characterized by distinctive straight lines of mortar joints. Mortar has several functions including holding the block in place, evenly distributing the weight,

THE WARRIOR AND HIS INTERGRITY

and providing protection from the external environment. These mortar functions are integrated into the wall, giving it integrity. As walls are integrated together they give a building integrity. The building can then be of useful service. If we simply stack brick to form a wall it will soon disintegrate like a "house of cards." Unfortunately, we often see this happen in the lives of people. Their lives are stacked like so many individual blocks, but there is no integrity, nothing that binds them, holds them together, keeps out evil influences, and makes them strong.

For a moment, consider character qualities like truthful, loyal, dependable, self-control, virtuous, courageous and compassionate. Consider how they could form a mortar for the building blocks of our lives. By integrating these and other qualities into our core, wholeness will be formed. Our lives could be held together by these Christ-like qualities giving us integrity, much like a well constructed wall. A strong family could be viewed as "walls of integrity," joined together to form a useful and vital structure, as our old pal Confucius pointed out.

In the military and in law enforcement, we wear layers of protection called Kevlar, sometimes called a ballistic vest. One layer of Kevlar offers very little protection from a serious threat. However, several layers will stop a deadly bullet. **Integrity is the spiritual warrior's Kevlar.** When we fail to cover and protect our hearts, we fall prey to evil influences and demonic forces. The more layers of Kevlar in a ballistic vest, the greater the protection for the one wearing it. In like manner, layers of character qualities such as courage, virtue and truthfulness can be integrated into our core, providing integrity, and protecting a cherished asset—our heart.

Look to Psalm 91 in its entirety as a guide to govern your thoughts and actions on the protection of your integrity. I call this the "Spiritual Kevlar—Plus" chapter. As a warrior, you should read it and meditate on it often. As you do so, ask God to show you more about the protection provided by integrity. Below is an Integrity Declaration that I developed for myself. Perhaps you too will find it useful.

Integrity Declaration:

Father God, I do not desire to be a fractionalized and divided man. I desire to be the whole and undivided man that you planned for me to be. I thank you that you loved me and gave your son Jesus as a ransom for me. I thank you that I can choose to follow Jesus, to imitate Him, to become like Him, to think like Him, to do like Him. I thank you Father, that your plan pieces my brokenness back together and makes me whole and undivided in my loyalties. I thank You that I am sealed by the Holy Spirit and that I am integrated into Your Kingdom as part of a holy edifice for Your glory. I thank you that I am not a collection of unrelated pieces but of an ongoing work of holy integration. I thank You that integrity protects my heart, guards my affections and that I am therefore a whole man prepared to serve You, my family and others with humility, with passion and with integrity. Integritas!

Chapter 19

THE WARRIOR AND HIS HONOR

Who sows virtue reaps honor.
Leonardo da Vinci (1452-1519)

I would lay down my life for America, but I cannot trifle with my honor.
John Paul Jones (1747-1792)

THE CONGRESSIONAL MEDAL OF HONOR

"For conspicuous gallantry and intrepidity at the risk of his life above and beyond the call of duty..."

These eighteen solemn words form the lead phrase on the great majority of citations, detailing the prerequisites for awarding the *Congressional Medal of Honor* (MOH). When spoken or read they profoundly resonate in one's spirit, detailing a concise and established set of preliminary criteria for induction into this hallowed band of warriors.

Part 3—The Warrior in Action / Warrior Qualities

For each of those individual citations, across the last 150 years the MOH has been authorized, you will find an American fighting man, one who suddenly faced overwhelming opposition with "conspicuous gallantry and intrepidity." Invariably the actions he chose to take were "at the risk of his own life." His incredible response to such adversity is in fact, "above and beyond the call of duty." His actions inflict great harm on the enemy, preserves the lives of his brothers nearby, and inspires those around him to charge on. His actions most often do result in his own death.

Three recent examples of such extraordinary sacrificial and heroic service are Navy SEAL Michael A. Monsoor, Army Specialist Ross A. McGinnis and Army Sergeant First Class Jared C. Monti who were all awarded the MOH posthumously in April 2008, June 2008 and September 2009 respectively.

One might ask, why do we call this highest of combat awards the Medal of Honor rather than the medal of exceptional valor, or the medal of unequaled gallantry? Although these are very apt titles, the answer is derived from the oft misunderstood definition of honor. The Webster's 1828 Dictionary defines honor as: (n.) *the esteem due or paid to worth; reverence.* And so, it is these intrepid and gallant acts of sacrificial service that have such great worth and value in preserving our traditions and way of life. They become cherished sagas in our national life experience.

Accordingly, these individual acts of heroism are so revered and of such consequence that our Congress has authorized the President to present the Medal of Honor to the heroic service member or his family as appropriate. In all of America's wars, subsequent to the War Between the States, there have only been 1945 awards of the MOH and at the time of this writing, only 82 recipients are living.

Honor in Our Culture

Honor however, has much more than a martial application and urgently needs to be infused throughout our culture. It is one of those essential precepts that, when properly understood and actively practiced, naturally strengthen personal, family and community relationships. Such a thread of honor, woven through our communities, will strengthen all aspects of our national life. Honor is a timeless bedrock value which transcends nationality and culture. I believe it should be a desired core value for every American and every Christian.

> HONOR IS A TIMELESS BEDROCK VALUE WHICH TRANSCENDS NATIONALITY AND CULTURE.

It saddens me that the distinguishing presence of that thread of honor, so painstakingly interwoven into the tapestry of our family, community and national life, has gotten a bit unraveled, somewhat frayed. Could it be that our use and understanding of our simple definition of honor *"the esteem due or paid to worth; reverence"* (noun) or *"to revere, to treat with deference, and respect"* (verb) has become blurred by the speed and pace by which we live?

I have carefully observed numerous aspects of American life pertaining to honor. I have also gained other anecdotal insight by asking individuals in each generation to give me their definition of honor. The normal response I get is not a definition at all. Rather, it is the name of an honorable action or concept such as *The Medal of Honor*, or standing when the judge enters the courtroom, or honoring God, parents, marriage and the American flag. Occasionally I will get a rather blank stare or a sheepish grin with downward glance. Regrettably, I seldom sense any significant degree of personal identification with the concept of honor. I believe this is linked to a lack of understanding of the word itself.

While the previous answers are all very good examples of appropriate objectives to be revered or honored, an actual definition is lacking. I believe the fundamental problem here is not that we have totally abandoned honor, but rather that we seem to have forgotten what honor actually is.

When we are careless with defining words, especially such cardinal precepts as honor, faith, love, or courage we can and do, with good intentions, substitute incorrect and revised terms. This weakens both our language and our culture. When you consider the word honor, either the verb or the noun form, what are some thoughts that come to your mind?

Values, Honor and Biblical Mandates

Perhaps of equal importance here is the whole issue of values, worth, and reverence. We should assess these in the context of what we honor, where honor should be given, and to whom we render honor. In my capacity as a senior law enforcement official, I often saw fellow human beings involved in completely dishonorable, depraved, perverted, or ignoble behaviors. Most of these actions are still illegal, at least in the state of South Carolina. Consequently, these people found themselves under arrest and in jail. As I reflect on this continual and ever increasing flow of errant humanity, I am reminded of Exodus 20.

The first few verses of this chapter contain the Ten Commandments. The first four of those commandments have to do with our vertical relationship—respecting and honoring God. The other six have to do with our horizontal relationships—respecting and honoring others. Of course Jesus succinctly unravels and simplifies all of this by boiling it down to two basic commands of Matthew 22:37-39. In paraphrase this would translate to, above all else love and honor God and secondarily love and honor others as you would yourself.

Part 3—The Warrior in Action / Warrior Qualities

For many years, criminologists have analyzed the complex issues of criminal behavior. I am familiar with much of their research, even as it continues today. An important clue to such behavior simply may be that as a culture, our giving of honor is misguided. We consistently esteem and revere the wrong people and things. As a culture, we prefer to honor the creature and associated creature comforts more than the Creator. As we survey modern American culture, it is obvious that a chief precursor to the erosion of respect and honor of constitutional and moral authority is the failure of people to honor and value biblical authority.

Numerous studies have carefully linked increased crime, teen pregnancy, illiteracy rates, and numerous other societal ills to specific Supreme Court decisions, some made a half a century ago. Removal of prayer in school, abortion on demand, and the continuing eradication of foundational Judeo-Christian values has resulted in a vastly diminished reverence for and honor of God in American culture. Amazingly, the historical fact is that reduced crime rates always occur during times of spiritual awakening.

This very issue was one of deep concern to many of our Founding Fathers. They, like da Vinci believed virtue and honor were mutually beneficial to mankind. James Madison, the primary author of the Constitution and our fourth President, said to the Virginia Assembly in 1778 "We have staked the whole future of American civilization, not upon the power of government, far from it. We have staked the future of all of our political institutions upon our capacity ... *to sustain themselves according to the Ten Commandments of God."*

In much the same manner John Adams, our second President and a major force in the founding of our nation, said this: "We have no government armed with power capable of contending with human passions unbridled by morality and religion." He went on to say..."Our Constitution is designed only for a moral and religious people. It is wholly inadequate for any other."

The Legacy of Honor

And for the support of this Declaration, with a firm reliance on the protection of divine Providence, we mutually pledge to each other our Lives, our Fortunes and our sacred Honor.

The Declaration of Independence, July 1776

It is imperative that we, individually and as a people, become very intentional in this whole process of rendering honor. First, if a holy, loving, merciful, and faithful God is of value and worth to you personally, then you must esteem, reverence and honor Him. Your attitude and actions toward God either honor or dishonor Him. As a people we honor God, simply by showing respect and obeying His commands. We also honor God by reading His Word often, by talking to Him daily, and by trusting Him with our lives.

Part 3—The Warrior in Action / Warrior Qualities

We honor God in the way we conduct our personal and professional affairs, the way we handle money, and how we treat and talk to others, both our families and friends, and those in the market places of life. Remember, Jesus said that if a person had done something "unto the least of these," they had in effect done that same thing to Him. It is essential that we purpose to build and leave a legacy of honor in our homes, at our work places, among our neighbors, and before God.

> WE HONOR GOD IN THE WAY WE CONDUCT OUR PERSONAL AND PROFESSIONAL AFFAIRS

What I have come to conclude is that by honoring and loving God in the macro, the result is that we begin honoring and loving others in the micro. We must resist the secular humanistic forces of our culture which dishonor the foundations of our nation and our faith. It is imperative that the unraveling and fraying of some of the relational threads of honor (those qualities that weave our families, communities, regions, and nation together,) be repaired.

Spiritual warriors must be men of honor, and we must act intentionally to render honor in all of our activities. If we are to be "One Nation Under God," we must be "One Nation Who Honors God." By so doing we can be useful instruments in restoring order and harmony in our culture. Perhaps ole' Leonardo was on to something when he said "who sows virtue reaps honor." Sowing virtue would seem to be a good place to start!

The warrior spirit is awakened and motivated by the challenge of a quest. The concept of being on the "tip of the spear" in a noble cause brings a twinkle to the eye, a stiffing of the spine, a resolute posture in the warrior's core. Such a quest is before us. It is to take up that thread of honor and become the "tip of the needle," weaving this sacred thread of honor back into the frayed tapestry of our culture. In the first chapter, *Born to be a Warrior*, we reviewed the exploits of the fabled knight Saint George and of his quest "to find work that only a knight can do." Restoring honor to our culture is certainly work that is worthy of the calling of a knight of the realm in the service of the King.

I believe that it is the Father's desire, one day to award the highest of all medals, even more everlasting than the revered *Medal of Honor*. On that day, when you individually answer your last call to muster before God, that He will be able to say to you, "Well done you good and faithful servant. Come on in!"

> Give everyone what you owe him
> ...if honor, then honor.
> Romans 13:7 a; d (NIV)

Part 3—The Warrior in Action / Warrior Qualities

Upon reading the excerpt below the warrior spirit may twinge a bit in regret for having not been one of those "happy few." In our quest of honor in a fallen culture, we often "appear" to be greatly outnumbered, as were these Englishmen recently landed in France. The "weakened" English army, outnumbered perhaps four to one, rallied on the day of battle with a resounding victory and with great honor. The French Army suffered thousands of casualties while the English lost less than 200.

"That he which hath no stomach for this fight,
Let him depart; his passport shall be made...
We would not die in that man's company
That fears his fellowship to die with us.
We few, we happy few, we band of brothers
For he to-day that sheds his blood with me
Shall be my brother, be he ne'er so vile,
This day shall gentle his condition;
And gentlemen in England now a-bed
Shall think themselves accursed they were not here,
And hold their manhoods cheap whiles any speaks
That fought with us upon Saint Crispin's day."

Henry's Speech at Agincourt (excerpts)
Wm. Shakespear (1564-1616)

"We few, we happy few, we band of brothers..." we have not missed our destiny. For this is the day of battle and we can also rally and fight for honor and for the KIng of kings, just as Henry fought valiantly side by side with his brothers, so does our King, and so much the more!

CHAPTER 20

THE WARRIOR AND HIS LOYALTY

Greater love has no man than this, than to lay down one's life for his friends. You are my friends if you do whatever I command you.

—Jesus of Nazareth

In our modern world of multi-tasking, competing priorities and exhaustive informational sound bites, this statement of Jesus may appear to come from another world. It does! Our computers do not store or process such information as unconditional love for others, or sacrificial service to others. In our culture, such concepts are no longer seen as being prerequisites for true relationships.

Our world is strangely uncomfortable with being commanded to do anything relational or anything not established as legal or contractual requirements. Yet, Jesus gives this timeless, compelling and voluntary standard for humankind to encounter, acknowledge and obey. It comes in an impactful manner that distinguishes it from those endless sound bites and mindless pop psychology. Perhaps it is that quality of simple truth that bypasses our

Part 3—The Warrior in Action / Warrior Qualities

heads and speaks to our hearts, that truth which grabs our undivided attention and demands a response.

Winston Churchill once said, "All great things are simple and many can be expressed in single words." Loyalty was not one of the six examples he used, but it certainly fits with the spirit of his quote. Loyalty really is a simple matter. It is a single word, but to measure its greatness is a monumental task. Suffice to say that the presence or absence of loyalty has preceeded the rise and fall of great nations, and of great men. The theme of loyalty and betrayal occupies center stage in the entire human drama, from Cain and Abel to the present day.

> All great things are simple and many can be expressed in single words.
>
> Winston Churchill

When I think of loyalty, one of the first examples that come to mind is that of Maggie, my three year old Rottweiler. Maggie, short for Magnolia Rose, is my very loyal friend. I assure you, the feeling is mutual. Loyalty, as we will discover, is a mutual transaction. As I am writing this piece, Maggie is asleep on the floor, just about four feet away.

Should I begin to roll my chair back from the computer, Maggie will raise her head, arch her ears and look at me with raw intensity, as if to say, "What do we do now, daddy?" With that animated expression she always conveys multiple thoughts—I'm ready; let's go; I really want to be where you are; please don't leave me! It takes no serious, deep thought here to grasp that the dog is a great model of loyalty God has given man for instruction. In fact, Maggie often shows me, in a very easy to comprehend manner, how I should relate to my Father God as well as to my family, friends, and other people.

According to Webster's 1828 Dictionary, loyalty (for people) is defined as: *Strong and enthusiastic sentiment accompanying a sense of allegiance to a sovereign, individual, or ideology. Faithful to —.* This definition reminds me of some dear Marine Corps friends, whose well-known motto is *Semper Fidelis,* Latin for "always faithful." In my experience, I have observed that being faithful is one of those inseparable, bonded partners of loyalty.

Loyalty has an almost sacred quality about it. It's a quality which transcends national and cultural boundaries, a core or heart issue. When exercised over time, it creates an environment of trust. Friends can build on it. It fosters a genuine love between partners that delights when they flourish and their associated enterprises prosper. Such trust-based relationships energize and strengthen any organization, be it corporate, military, church, government, or family.

I define the warrior spirit as **the passionate desire and determination in the heart of a man, a desire to perfect himself for the stance against evil in the service to others.**

PART 3—THE WARRIOR IN ACTION / WARRIOR QUALITIES

This warrior spirit is in fact, a companion spirit of loyalty. In the context of a pure warrior, loyalty is a quality that is assumed to be present. Sadly, that is not always the case. This fact may have prompted the great warrior, General George S. Patton, to make this observation. *"There is a great deal of talk about loyalty from the bottom to the top. Loyalty from the top down is even more necessary and much less prevalent."* In a somewhat related comment the General also said. *"I prefer a loyal staff officer to a brilliant one."* Having both been a staff officer, and commanded a staff myself, I say a hearty, Amen!

As Patton so clearly stated, loyalty is not something that a leader will automatically get, like a tax or tribute from a subordinate. **Rather, loyalty should always be a mutual transaction.** General Patton clearly gave, in the realm of natural war, an enduring example of the principle that you cannot expect loyalty without demonstrating loyalty. His storied Third Army certainly embodied the spirit of loyalty. This loyalty became manifest in the strength of their shared trust, love and faithfulness to one another and to their unprecedented battlefield successes.

LOYALTY AND THE CHRISTIAN WARRIOR

In the spiritual realm, our Lord Christ demonstrated the highest order of loyalty. He was not only the consummate warrior-leader for our cause, He was the point man on every patrol. He was undaunted by intense opposition. His complete obedience to Father God and His passionate love and loyalty toward us led Him to approach and take a prominent hill—Calvary.

In so doing, our Lord personally defined for all time, the ultimate standard of love, and bi-directional loyalty, expressed by Paul in Romans 5:8b,...*while we were still sinners, Christ died for us.* (NKJV) He was loyal to His Father, maintaining his undeterred commitment to the Father's directives. He was also utterly loyal to us, laying down His life in self-sacrifice and service to humankind. When we read this familiar passage, we see that true loyalty is nurtured and motivated by love. Experience has taught me that love and loyalty are inseparable forces, both in our professional lives and in our personal lives.

An excellent example of the loyalty/love dynamic is recorded in John 21:15-23. Although a familiar passage to many, I believe it is worthy of some discussion. This passage describes a point that I, and probably most men, have come to from time to time. Please read it over now to refresh your memory.

What we usually remember about this passage is that Jesus had to explain something to Peter three times. This was necessary to get Peter to understand that it was *agápe*, or unconditional love, that he must have in order to complete his mission to *"feed my sheep."* This high standard of love was necessary for Peter to muster the necessary loyalty and obedience to fulfill his spiritual warrior calling.

Part 3—The Warrior in Action / Warrior Qualities

It is all too easy to miss the implications of verse 18, please read it again. Jesus reminded Peter with powerful descriptive language that the road ahead would not be a cake walk. In fact, the verse ends with a description of the type of death Peter would face should loyalty and obedience be his chosen path. Having gone through the requirements once more with Peter, Jesus simply gives him that great military command: *"Follow Me!"*

At this point another valuable lesson on loyalty is given, one that can benefit us all. Peter was not yet fully on board with the "follow me" program. He still had some questions and asked Jesus (verse 21) about *"the one who betrays You?"* Every pastor, ministry leader and parent needs to be familiar with verse 22. Let me paraphrase what Jesus said. Son, that is above your pay grade. In other words, that is of no concern to you. Jesus clarifies Peter's strategic imperative even more, saying (in paraphrase), You, Peter, are not to be concerned about anyone's loyalty but your own. Jesus finally gives Peter some directive loving guidance, *"You follow Me."* No parsing of words here.

Again, I think Peter's struggle with love, loyalty and spiritual warfare is a graphic demonstration to we spiritual warriors and the path we travel. Here is a fisherman who walked away from his business and enthusiastically followed Jesus for three years of discipleship. In the Garden of Gethsemane, Peter slipped backward into the natural realm of his flesh and his raw emotion. First, he fell asleep three times after being told by Jesus "to watch and pray" (Mark 14:37). Peter seemed to be one of those guys who needs three strikes but is still allowed to stay in the batter's box. There is a great message here for we who lead warriors.

When confronted with physical force, Peter drew his sword and cut off the ear of Malchus, a servant of the High Priest. Wow! Some would say, "outstanding hand and eye coordination." I would have to agree. Finally, just a short time later, Peter infamously denied that he even knew Jesus. Again, he got three strikes but stayed at bat. I, for one can identify with Peter's journey.

Developing a Loyalty Index

Have you ever heard of a loyalty seminar or loyalty listed as a college course or Bible study? Perhaps that would be a good discipleship subject to pursue. I once even contemplated developing a "loyalty index" that would be some sort of matrix by which I could assess and predict the loyalty of staff. Over time, I have come to conclude that loyalty is not a classroom subject, because it is such a heart issue. However, it must be presented, discussed and heralded as an essential quality. In such an atmosphere,

> LOYALTY IS NOT A CLASSROOM SUBJECT, BECAUSE IT IS SUCH A HEART ISSUE.

Part 3—The Warrior in Action / Warrior Qualities

loyalty is more likely to become a part of the culture—business, government, church, family, etc.

In reality, the only way to test and know the "loyalty index" of people is to go through some challenging or difficult times with them. It is only on the other side of the storm that you discover who is loyal, who you can count on, who you can trust—who remains in the boat. Loyalty is an essential ingredient in all trust-based relationships, not just on the battlefield of natural war.

> IT IS ONLY ON THE OTHER SIDE OF THE STORM THAT YOU DISCOVER WHO IS LOYAL.

A very practical way for the warrior to check his loyalty is by how he responds to decisions made by his authority, like Jesus in dealing with Peter. There may be opportunity to have input into command decisions, but once the decision is made by the person in authority, it must be embraced by the loyal warrior, just as though it were their own personal decision. Anything less is disloyal, even seditious—like Judas' actions. If left unchecked, disloyalty can weaken and endanger an entire enterprise. I do believe Peter finally got there, and that his journey should be a resource for modern spiritual warriors and their leaders to study.

THE WARRIOR AND HIS LOYALTY

I have felt the biting sting of betrayal, twice by subordinates, one of whom I cared for deeply. This sting once came from a commanding officer, who I personally liked, but who was governed by politics. Such betrayals do happen. They hurt, too. **They almost always come unannounced and create significant emotional and spiritual challenges.** They may occur in your professional life, as mine did, or within your family, your church, or your community life. They may even rise up in your relationships with friends. John 21:21-22 is a good place to begin to regain your perspective and to get on with your own "follow me" program. As Jesus finally told Peter, "You Follow Me!" I just wish that I had known that back in '83. It would probably have been a great help.

As spiritual warriors, and as leaders of spiritual warriors, we need to drink often from the well of love and loyalty. We need to be refreshed by the simplicity of these attributes. We need to often review the maxim that the "unity of the brethren" (e.g. Psalm 133, John 17:11, Ephesians 4:3) is top priority with God. In fact, unit cohesion (unity,) an oft cited martial standard is simply God's order. It is good. It is pleasant. It is refreshing and builds strength. It stimulates harmony and produces fruit. Most of all, unity is transformative in nature. Is not that our goal?

Through the crucible of selfless, sacrificial service the loyal warrior is transformed into the image of Christ. Like Peter, this must be our overall *strategic imperative*.

Part 3—The Warrior in Action / Warrior Qualities

The writer of Hebrews gives us a convenient reservoir to drink from in chapter 12:1-3. Loyalty, as Peter discovered, is not a quick sprint. It is a marathon, requiring tenacity and endurance. This passage reminds us that Jesus has readily supplied the highest order of love and loyalty to Father God and to us. Remember, we identified this somewhat rare quality as "bi-directional" loyalty. The spiritual warrior must always be conscious of this standard, to be loyal both upward and downward.

The top-down loyalty that is "more necessary," as General Patton so well demonstrated in the natural warfare realm, has been so much more abundantly supplied to us in the spiritual warfare realm by our Lord Christ. Therefore, the spiritual warrior's response must be akin to the warriors of Patton's Third Army. In this we are left without excuse because, as we discovered, loyalty must be a mutual transaction.

> *For consider Him who endured such hostility from sinners against Himself, lest you become weary and discouraged in your souls.*
> Hebrews 12:3 (NKJV)

Semper Fidelis!

CHAPTER 21

THE WARRIOR AND HIS COURAGE

Be on your guard; stand firm in the faith; be men of courage; be strong.

1 Corinthians 16:13 (NIV)

Courage is rightly esteemed the first of human qualities because it is the quality which guarantees all others.

Sir Winston Churchill (1874-1965)

Courage, n. [L., cor heart.] Bravery; intrepidity; that quality of mind which enables men to encounter danger and difficulties with firmness, or without fear or depression of spirits; valor; boldness; resolution (Webster's 1828).

Courage is derived from the Latin word cor which means "heart." It is important to notice that this is the root word for core and coronary. Courage then is fundamentally an issue of the heart. Indeed, it is much more a spiritual force than a cerebral process. Later on we will discuss personal courage in some detail.

Acts of personal courage strongly influence the attitudes and conduct of others around us. Billy Graham, the noted Christian leader, made this observation: *"Courage is contagious. When a brave man takes a stand, the spines of others are often stiffened."* A courageous act often serves to demonstrate that life, or at least certain aspects of life, have such intrinsic value that personal sacrifice is sometimes required to preserve and protect them. Having said that, I do believe that courage is one of the most misunderstood as well as misused core words in our modern lexicon.

Defining Courage

If you were asked to describe a personal act of courage or to define a courageous action, to whom or what would you refer? Perhaps you would suggest a New York City fire fighter or police officer, whose individual action on September 11, 2001 was universally accepted as courageous and heroic. Another likely response could be found in the actions of an American soldier, engaged in close combat with the enemy in the current War on Terror. The reality is that acts of courage, as defined by Webster, are to be found all around us.

We often learn about "average citizen heroes" and their incredible acts of courage as part of a broader story of human tragedy. Of course, one prominent example of this recurring theme is woven throughout the tragic events of 9/11, at the Twin Towers, the Pentagon and

THE WARRIOR AND HIS COURAGE

the crash site in Pennsylvania. As I write this, we have just observed the 10th anniversary of that precursor of so many significant events of this past decade. Virtually any American over the age of twenty remembers exactly what they were doing when the twin towers fell.

We also recall many heroic acts of courage associated with this tragedy. In this process we must also be reminded of the faith by which many others were reported to have lived their lives. Prior to offering themselves in selfless acts of service and sacrifice, courage was part of their core. For most of us, the memories of those horrendous acts are also seared into our consciousness. Perhaps a review of some of the inspirational acts of courage by "average citizen heroes" will inspire us, even while honoring them.

One such act was led by Todd Beamer, a thirty-two year old father of two, who was aboard the hijacked Flight 93. This flight was, in all likelihood, directed toward The White House. Instead, it crashed into a Pennsylvania field. You may recall that Todd, realizing the danger they were facing, quickly developed a plan and gathered a band of fellow passengers to help. Their actions—to retake the plane or crash it—were initiated by the now celebrated command *"Let's roll."* This remarkable act of courage, in all likelihood, saved countless lives, prevented a much broader disarray of our national government, and surely helped to preserve our way of life. It also gave our troops a ferocious war cry as they fight the continuing war on terror, "Let's Roll!"

"LET'S ROLL!"

PART 3—THE WARRIOR IN ACTION / WARRIOR QUALITIES

Todd's devoted widow, Lisa, authored a best-selling book entitled <u>Let's Roll: Ordinary People Extraordinary Courage</u> (a great read,) which has impacted and inspired several hundred thousand people. On September 11, 2001 Todd Beamer's reservoir of courage and his undaunted spirit determined his response to the horrific situation developing around him. Perfectly fulfilling the definition of courage, he has become enshrined as an "ordinary hero" in the hearts of all who love liberty and freedom. His actions epitomized a courageous warrior.

Another "ordinary hero" rose to the challenge in the spring of 2007. The whole world became aware of the gallantry and courage of a seventy-six year old Holocaust survivor, Liviu Librescu. You may recall that Professor Librescu was teaching his class of students at Virginia Tech on the morning of April 16. The elderly professor had devoted his life to scientific research and teaching young people. For the previous twenty years he had been on the campus of Virginia Tech, where he was loved, admired and respected by all.

After hearing gunshots and screams from the adjacent classroom, the elderly professor quickly directed his students to flee out of classroom windows to safety. Rather than attempt to save his own life, this devoted engineering and mathematics professor chose to save others. He made the courageous decision to become a human shield between the approaching danger and his own students, thus offering himself as a sacrifice for others.

In the horrible aftermath, Professor Librescu's body was found lying across the entrance to his classroom. However, all of his students were found to be alive. Ironically, he chose to demonstrate this greatest act of love on the Israeli Holocaust Remembrance Day. He was buried as a hero the next day in his beloved Israel. Liviu Librescu had survived the many dangers of a Nazi death camp and the brutal Romanian Communist Party.

In the face of great adversity, Liviu Librescu obeyed once more, the ancient command of Joshua *chazaq v' amats*—be strong and of good courage. We must somehow remember such heroic acts of courage and retell them, rather than dwell on the tragedy and related victimology, as some are prone to do.

THE RESULTS OF COURAGEOUS ACTS

"Courage is not simply one of the virtues...but the form of every virtue at its testing point."

C. S. Lewis

As we focus on our own personal courage, I believe it is very important to ponder a thought that you may have missed along your way. How truly tragic and meaningless life would be if it were not for such demonstrations of courage in the midst of life's most challenging circumstances. I have observed that when courage is demonstrated in relation to a particular tragic, traumatic, or challenging human event that it serves to mitigate

Part 3—The Warrior in Action / Warrior Qualities

the impact of related trauma. Sometimes a courageous response prevents an even greater tragedy from playing out. Courage in our heart is a reservoir from which we can draw strength to face our own challenges, fears and difficulties which we know intuitively lie ahead.

We must all be prepared to act with courage, because we all face dangerous, difficult, or unpleasant situations at some point. The dangers or fears you will face may not be Islamic terrorists hijacking your plane, or mad gunmen shooting people all around you. They may be damaged relationships, health or financial crises, or serious family tragedies. Personal courage, drawn from those internal reservoirs of strength, will be required to face such moments that you encounter along your way.

> WE MUST ALL BE PREPARED TO ACT WITH COURAGE.

Mettle (strength of character) is an often used synonym for courage. Cowardice is the lack of courage and the antonym for it. While testing people's mettle is not quite the same as testing their courage, I have found that in both instances the test comes unannounced. We must be prepared, and have a mind set to exercise our mettle and act with courage when we come face to face with "testy" situations. In the very real issues of life there really is no middle ground. We either act with courage or we act with cowardice.

I have studied extensively the life and career of General George S. Patton, one of history's greatest battlefield

THE WARRIOR AND HIS COURAGE

generals. He, like many military leaders spoke of two types of courage. Physical courage is that quality which enables a soldier to face bullets in battle. Moral courage is that which enables a soldier to stand up for what he believes in and knows is right. Of moral courage General Patton said this: "Moral courage is the most valuable and usually the most absent characteristic in men."

> MORAL COURAGE IS THAT WHICH ENABLES A SOLDIER TO STAND UP FOR WHAT HE BELIEVES IN.

I found that to be a shocking statement. As a naval officer, I was evaluated annually. One of the areas of evaluation and grading was moral courage, defined as "response in stressful situations." Warriors must consistently expect of ourselves an "A" rating in this vital area—nothing less. *Chazaq v' amats!* Be strong and of good courage!

Moses and Joshua were both great leaders who faced many difficult and dangerous situations. In contrasting them, Moses seemed to be concerned with actions that would protect the people from danger. Joshua seemed to be concerned with actions that would prepare the people to face danger. *Amats*, translated courage, initially appears in Numbers 13:20, *be of good courage and bring some fruit of the land* (NKJV).

This word was directed at twelve leaders, one selected from each tribe of Israel. They were formed into a twelve man recon team. The team, you may recall, spent forty days gathering intel about the territory God was giving Israel. Sadly, only Caleb of the tribe of Judah, and Joshua of the tribe of Ephriam demonstrated *amats*. Ten leaders showed cowardice and we know the result.

Interestingly, the term courage is never applied to Moses. Although God spoke the term to Moses, who was obviously a very courageous man, it was always directed through Moses to Joshua. I believe the directive nature of this discourse is why Joshua emphasized to the people that they would be facing significant adversity.

There was an emerging requirement for all to *chazaq v' amats*—be strong and of good courage. Courage was a new term, a new mandate if you will. It was obviously a necessary quality for all Israelites to face and conquer what now lay before them. It was not just for Moses and Joshua alone. **In today's American Church there is a danger of having a Moses mindset, to "protect from adversity," rather than a Joshua mindset, to "prepare for adversity."** Joshua's was a conquering mindset. Ponder that a moment.

Courage is neither braggadocio nor arrogance. It is certainly more than a positive mental attitude. Courage is the substance that fills a holy warrior's heart, creating an internal reservoir of strength from which to draw when facing adversity and difficulties. Courage is that internalized motivation to face and deal with dangerous, difficult, or unpleasant situations. Courage prevents a man from capitulating and surrendering to the adversary, or to the adversity he faces. *Chazaq v' amats!*

THE WARRIOR AND HIS COURAGE

Cowards die many times before their deaths;
the valiant never taste of death but once.

Wm. Shakespeare, Julius Caesar II

Be strong and of good courage...that you may prosper wherever you go.

Joshua 1:6-7 (NKJV)

Courage is almost a contradiction in terms. It means a strong desire to live taking the form of a readiness to die. 'He that will lose his life, the same shall save it.' A soldier surrounded by his enemy, if he is to cut his way out, needs to combine a strong desire for living with a strong carelessness about dying. He must not merely cling to life, for then he will be a coward, and will not escape. He must not merely wait for death, for then he will be a suicide, and will not escape. He must seek his life in a furious indifference to it; he must desire life like water and yet drink death like wine.

-G.K. Chesterson

Part 3—The Warrior in Action / Warrior Qualities

"We were made to be courageous
We were made to lead the way
We could be the generation
That finally breaks the chains...

We were warriors on the front lines
Standing unafraid
But now we're watchers on the side lines
While our families slip away

Where are you, men of courage?
You were made for so much more
Let the pounding of our hearts cry
We will serve the Lord...

The only way we'll ever stand
Is on our knees with lifted hands
Make us courageous
Lord, make us courageous...

We will re-ignite the passion
That we buried deep inside
Let the men of God arise
We were made to be courageous...

Excerpts Courageous,
performed by Casting Crowns.
Lyrics written by
Matthew West and Mark Hall"

PART THREE

THE WARRIOR IN ACTION/WARRIOR QUALITIES

Thoughts for Individual Reflection or Group Discussion

Chapter 16

1. Discuss the concept of exercising authority.

2. Describe the proper exercise of authority and how it applies to you.

3. Discuss the Centurion's understanding of authority from Luke 7.

4. Discuss the relationship of discipleship to the exercise of authority.

Part 3—The Warrior in Action / Warrior Qualities

Chapter 17

1. Discuss the sword as a weapon of war and a symbol of authority.

2. Discuss the concept that the weapon is an extension of the warrior.

3. Discuss how the "holy warrior" becomes proficient with his "sword."

4. Discuss the likely outcome when unskilled warriors stumble onto the battlefield.

Chapter 18

1. Describe the relationship between integrity, disintegrate, and integrate.

2. How are oaths, vows and contracts related to integrity?

3. Relate how integrity protects your heart as the legionnaire's armor protected his.

4. Discuss how the Integrity Declaration can be of value to the Christian warrior.

THOUGHTS FOR REFLECTION OR GROUP DISCUSSION

Chapter 19

1. What is the definition of honor? Why is it important in the 21st century?

2. Discuss the relationship of virtue to honor.

3. What are some ways that we honor God? …honor family? …honor our heritage?

4. Discuss some ways to restore honor where there has been dishonor.

Chapter 20

1. What is your definition of loyalty?

2. Discuss: Loyalty, an issue of the heart or of the head?

3. Discuss bi-directional loyalty.

4. Discuss the dynamic of love and loyalty between Peter and Jesus in John 21: 15-23.

Part 3—The Warrior in Action / Warrior Qualities

Chapter 21

1. Discuss the meaning of courage.

2. Discuss an act of courage that you know of personally.

3. Explain the difference between moral and physical courage.

4. Discuss the Moses mindset vs. the Joshua mindset with regard to facing danger.

PART FOUR

WARRIOR LEADERSHIP AND WARRIOR VALUES

Part 4—Warrior Leadership and Warrior Values

> WE MUST TAKE ON CHRIST'S NATURE AND HIS CHARACTER. THEN, WE CAN PROPERLY EXERCISE THE AUTHORITY THAT HE HAS ALREADY GIVEN US.

Chapter 22

THE WARRIOR AS A LEADER: XENOPHON AND JESUS

GUIDANCE FOR 21ST CENTURY HOLY WARRIORS

The true test of a leader is whether his followers will adhere to his cause from their own volition, enduring the most arduous hardships without being forced to do so, and remaining steadfast in the moments of greatest peril.

There is small risk a general will be regarded with contempt by those he leads, if whatever he may have to preach, he shows himself best able to perform.

It is highly indicative of good leadership when people obey someone without coercion...

—Xenophon 430-354 B.C.

PART 4—WARRIOR LEADERSHIP AND WARRIOR VALUES

*Whoever does not take up their cross
and follow me is not worthy of me;
Whoever wants to be my disciple
must deny themselves and take up their cross
and follow me;
Follow me and let the dead
bury their own dead;
Anyone who loves their life will lose it,
while anyone who hates their life in this world
will keep it for eternal life;
Greater love has no one than this:
to lay down one's life for one's friends;
My sheep know my voice
and will not follow a stranger.*

—Jesus Christ (NIV excerpts)

ANCIENT LEADER PERSPECTIVES

Xenophon and Jesus are not often mentioned in the same sentence. In fact, this may be the first time ever. However, as leaders, their precepts have much in common that is worthy of examination and review by leaders today. In my view it is further evidence of the virtual seamless nature of natural warfare and spiritual warfare.

The Warrior as a Leader: Xenophon and Jesus

Of the more explicit consistencies in their expectations is that danger, personal sacrifice, and even death could be encountered, simply by following them. However, coercion or any hint of manipulating followers or exploiting their emotions to gain their loyalty, or simply to complete an objective, would be antithetical to the thinking both of Jesus and of Xenophon.

Although Xenophon is revered for his leadership and scholarship rather than his spiritual qualities, he recognized that the best approach to attaining an objective was "to turn the soul of people toward some noble purpose." Ponder that. Both he and Plato were ardent students of Socrates, the ancient sage who uncovered many truths regarding the nature of man and of creation.

Some knowledge of their scholarship is helpful in understanding events in our natural world today. Our Founding Fathers understood this. They were schooled in the principles of Natural Law from which our Western Culture and institutions draw heavily. Natural Law, as espoused by Cicero some 300 years after Xenophon, had its origins in the thought of Socrates and his students, Xenophon being one.

It was Socrates who gave us "the unexamined life is not worth living," and Plato gave the familiar "Necessity is the mother of invention." Xenophon expresses an insightful grasp of some of their core thought in the quotations describing the ideal leader. A concise understanding of leadership, this most critical component of creation and

Part 4—Warrior Leadership and Warrior Values

human activity, must be preceded by an understanding of the nature of man. In fact, by defining the ideal leader our old pal Xenophon perfectly described Jesus Christ. Ponder that thought!

Xenophon believed the reliance upon force to gain the compliance of followers to perform any task is tyranny, including that which anticipates extraordinary personal sacrifice. Such conduct by those in authority toward their followers reduces people to the level of beasts. This type of rule, compelling and manipulating people to do your bidding, is a deviation from nature. His response to such behavior: "Such conduct belongs to those who have strength without judgment."

To help resolve this issue the ancients developed the pietho (persuasion) and the bia (force) precept. Keep in mind this was before The Father sent us Jesus, so we could clearly see the ideal leader in action. Xenophon would say that persuasion (pietho) was the natural medium for a leader to influence human beings, since humans were separated from animals by the gift of reason.

Force (bia), the absence of reason, was the way of the tyrant, because it was unnatural for people and fitting only for beasts. Perhaps this is why, at some points in my professional career, as well as in church life, I have felt I was caught up in a cattle drive, a driven creature complete with the sting of a cattle prod…ouch!

THE WARRIOR AS A LEADER: XENOPHON AND JESUS

LEADERSHIP—A SACRED ART

I must say, I believe that leadership is a sacred art. Leaders in general have a sacred duty for both vertical and horizontal accountability and responsibility. It is not readily apparent that this concept has wide acceptance or understanding in our American culture, as the case once was. In both my professional life and my church life, I have experienced a broad spectrum of leadership styles. Most have been inspirational and motivational. Others have been just the opposite. Your experience may have been similar to some degree.

The fact is that our nation and our world are reeling from leaders at many levels of authority who have no moral compass and absolutely no sense of sacred duty. This lack is apparent in almost every sector. Their ranks are often filled with coerced and manipulated followers. It saddens me to say that the church is not immune from such inept leadership practices.

Those of us in leadership need to periodically examine ourselves to discover how "Xenophonesque" we are as leaders. Better still, how "Jesusesque" we are. Paul gave us the standard: "imitate me just as I also imitate Christ" (1 Corinthians 4:16 NKJV). Paul uses the

> "IMITATE ME JUST AS I ALSO IMITATE CHRIST"
>
> PAUL THE APOSTLE

Part 4—Warrior Leadership and Warrior Values

word *mimeomai*, from which we derive our word mimic. This word carries with it a powerful concept: decisive action with permanent results.

Are you willing to hold yourself and free your followers to abide by that standard? ...including family? If so, how will you know when you miss the mark? Who among your followers has the freedom and influence to tell you? Part of such examination must include a fearless inventory of the source of our own motivations to get things done. Do we coerce or manipulate the people? Do we drive them like beasts? Or, do they freely and willingly follow, as sheep naturally do. During your fearless inventory be sure to check for cattle prods.

Xenophon "walked his talk" when he joined 10,000 Greek mercenaries following Cyrus, from Greece, deep into Asia Minor. During the march, the Greeks discovered they had been deceived by Cyrus regarding their objective. The Greeks balked, but after much coercion they marched on. But during the ensuing Battle of Cunaxa, Cyrus was killed. After some further intrigue and betrayal, the Greek army found itself cutoff deep in enemy territory, 1000 miles from home. Because of his character, the Greek army elected Xenophon to lead them. Ponder that! The 10,000, as they are known to history, fought their way north to the Black Sea. Some 4000 Greeks were killed in this epic march out of Mesopotamia, giving their lives willingly in pursuit of a noble purpose.

JESUS—THE COMPLETE LEADER

Jesus Christ is the consummate leader. We all surely must know that. Perhaps this brief discussion of leadership, and of Xenophon, will temper and sharpen your own understanding of yourself and your awareness of your followers. Both Jesus and Xenophon led from the front. Both were followed by people pursuing a noble purpose at their own volition. Jesus still is.

As leaders, our main role is to serve them, leading them to follow Him, the one who confidently commanded "Follow Me!" In so doing we practice the sacred art of leadership, modeling the noble nature of followership. The question before you is this. What will you do? Will you turn the soul of those you lead toward some noble purpose?

Part 4 — Warrior Leadership and Warrior Values

> "The reliance upon force to gain the compliance of followers to perform any task is tyranny."
>
> — Xenophon

CHAPTER 23

THE LIONSHIP OF LEADERSHIP

A Message for Warriors on Leadership

Leadership is a potent combination of strategy and character. But if you must be without one, be without the strategy.
General H. Norman Schwarzkopf

An army of sheep led by a lion is to be more feared than an army of lions led by a sheep.
Chabrais (415 BC-357 BC)

I have had the great pleasure of traveling to Kenya on two occasions, both times as a Naval Officer. Kenyans are generally a very happy, friendly people, and are tremendous hosts. Kenya is also the natural home for flourishing populations of African wildlife, and an

Part 4—Warrior Leadership and Warrior Values

abundance of absolutely spectacular and unforgettable vistas, among them the stunning Mount Kilimanjaro. Tsavo, one of several national parks, is larger than New Jersey and contains numerous varieties of animal herds. It also is populated by thriving and abundant prides of lion. It was in Tsavo that I twice experienced the unique thrill and excitement of safari.

For years I have been fascinated by the lion, panthera leo—The King of Beasts. Through the centuries these magnificent creatures have been symbols for honor, courage and authority. In my view, the male lion is also the obvious choice to be the animal symbol of the warrior spirit. In Scripture, Jesus is referred to as "the Lion of the Tribe of Judah." Think about that for a moment. Of all the animals, the Holy Spirit inspired John to identify Jesus with the lion.

You may have watched a television documentary portraying a pride of twelve to twenty lions. Believe me, no documentary comes close to capturing the sensations of personally being near a pride. The commanding roar of the male lion is said to audible for up to five miles. So, when you are within forty to fifty yards of one, he has your complete attention. This is especially true if you are armed with only a survival knife, a camera and mosquito repellant.

Male lions lead in the same manner in 2011 as they have throughout history. They seem to understand the authority they possess by virtue of being lions. This

The Lionship of Leadership

concept is manifest through the leadership they walk out on a daily basis in front of other lions, as well as all other animals. The males seem to realize intuitively that their mere presence, or even the distant silhouette of their great mane, brings a sense of security to the pride. It also strikes fear, or at least great respect in the heart of every other animal.

It would seem that a mature male lion, a true warrior, and probable victor in the conflicts of life, fully understands the role of authority and its unique relationship to leadership. To become a leader among lions requires a bit more than training, tenure, and a strong résumé. In short, the leader of the pride has "influenced others, and has obtained their obedience, respect, confidence, and loyal cooperation in the pursuit of a task or objective." This, incidentally, is a definition of leadership I developed many years ago. It seems to fit here very well.

Observing a pride of lion is a picture of beauty, order and symmetry. The males, lying or standing out in the open, regally poised, are stunning portrayals of kingship and kingdom. Their very presence enables lion cubs to play in safety, as well as mature into functional adult lions, both male and female.

It is a remarkable result of God's plan, that by fulfilling their pre-ordained role in their sphere of authority, order is established. The lioness is free to go "shopping" for food without fear of being mugged,

Part 4—Warrior Leadership and Warrior Values

> **The daughter of a lion must understand that she too is a lion.**
> African Proverb

and she can nurture her young in complete safety. The lioness also operates in a critical role of authority under the male covering. A related African proverb states, "the daughter of a lion must understand that she too is a lion."

A mature male lion seems to know that his "Lionship" is necessary for the preservation of order. He knows that a proliferation of effeminate male lions (should there be such a thing,) would lead to the dethronement of lions as the "King of Beasts." He comprehends that there is a purpose for leadership and authority. This is why weaker, young males have a rough time finding employment as leaders of lion prides.

This is the principle warriors must know: **If any kingdom is to survive and thrive, the king must produce heirs who will carry on the rule of that kingdom!** Pause just a moment, and consider the spiritual application of that fact. In the lion kingdom that purpose is to provide for a peaceable, functional, and thriving pride of lions. In short, this prevents the jackals and hyenas from taking over.

Hopefully this leaves you a bit challenged in your thinking as well as inspired and motivated mentally and spiritually. As Christian men in America, we are in need of being transformed, as Paul exhorts us in 2 Corinthians 3:18 and Romans 12:2. We are to take on the image of the "Lion of the Tribe of Judah." This means we must take on Christ's nature and His character. Then, we can properly exercise the authority that He has already given us. The male lions on the grand open savannas of Tsavo do, in many ways, provide us with highly effective role models.

As men, and particularly as fathers and grandfathers, we must let the hyenas and jackals know that the King's authority is being exercised and administered in the realms where we roam. There are many fatherless young men (cubs) who need a "father lion's shadow" under which they can play and grow, and to whom they can look for a model. There is such a great need for quality mentors today (See 1 Corinthians 4:15).

As fathers and leaders, our families should be comforted and assured simply by being in our presence. Let's continue to man up and be fully transformed into the image of the "Lion of the Tribe of Judah." Such warriors are the main defense for families, the church and communities in keeping the hyenas and jackals at bay.

Part 4—Warrior Leadership and Warrior Values

> Character is like a tree and reputation like a shadow. The shadow is what we think of it, the tree is the real thing.
>
> —Abraham Lincoln

> The will to win compares little with the will to prepare to win.
>
> —Coach Paul "Bear" Bryant

CHAPTER 24

THE WARRIOR AND HIS CORE VALUES

I hope I shall always possess firmness and virtue enough to maintain what I consider the most enviable of all titles, the character of an honest man.
George Washington

Core, n. [L., cor heart.] The central part of or the heart of something such as the core of fruit or the heart of timber. The essence of; the inmost part.
Webster's Dictionary

Core values are the cardinal precepts or tenets held by organizations or individuals. They are a small set of essential maxims which serve to mold and guide individual or corporate conduct as they are identified with and followed. Though some would argue that character and core values are one and the same, I do not. I have

Part 4 - Warrior Leadership and Warrior Values

found that a functional identity with specific core values is of indispensable value to me. It allows me to refine and strengthen various character qualities in my personal and professional life.

Anyone can google "core values" and find a variety of web offerings on the subject. For instance, you can find the published core values for many corporations, for the various military services, for individual churches, denominations, law enforcement agencies, universities and other organizations. In most cases core values are listed, along with an explanation of each one. The Army has seven listed core values; the Navy and Air Force each have only three, but not the same three.

If you cannot readily articulate your personal core values, I encourage you to prayerfully explore various web sites to evaluate those of truly significant organizations. You can even find web sites dedicated to assisting you in identifying your core values.

The Essence of Core Values

I am a curious person by nature and often invite individuals to share their core values with me. It is a valuable relationship builder, although it must be done in an appropriate manner. More often than not I am confronted with a guarded response. However, with a little prompting, words like integrity or truthful or patriotic emerge. In a former professional capacity I made the final decision regarding many applicants for various

The Warrior and His Core Values

law enforcement positions. The subject of core values was always purposefully visited.

During one particular interview, when asked about core values, the applicant confidently gave me his seven core values. These included honor, courage, loyalty, and self-less service. I knew from his application that he was a sergeant in the National Guard. I also recognized these to be the Army's core values.

More importantly, I was impressed with his familiarity, identity with, and comfort level with them. The applicant explained that these were not just idle words. They were powerful concepts which had served him well in combat as well as a family man. I offered him a position on the spot!

Not long after this interview, I was thinking about core values and happened to be eating my daily apple, a very tasty Red Delicious. As I came to the core, I realized that the core of an apple was more than the physical center. I guess I had an epiphany. The core is really the essence of the apple, for buried deep inside were the seeds. These few seeds carried the potential to produce many apple trees. I realized that the one apple I had just enjoyed eating could do much more than keep the doctor away for one day, for just one person.

I could see the apple and apple core being somewhat analogous to the applicant and his core values. He could do much more that fill a position as a deputy sheriff. Accordingly, an understanding of core values can bring

Part 4 - Warrior Leadership and Warrior Values

a greater sense of purpose and meaning into our lives, both individually and corporately. Our core values contain the seeds that will produce fruit, either good fruit or bad fruit.

Values of the Heart

Core comes to us from the Latin root word "cor" which literally means heart. It is interesting to note that the words courage and coronary are derived from the same root. It follows then that core values are not obtained by intellectual assent. Rather, they are deeply held heart issues. Core values actually do define our core, not only what we ought to be, but what we can be. They point us to who we must be, and in reality who we are. They require no external justification. They stand alone as intrinsic values to guide us, and silent sentinels to guard our thoughts and actions.

> For the warrior, core values such as honor, courage, loyalty, and selfless service resonate deeply within.

Some may scoff at or mock those who espouse good core values. They may even say that they are just some idle, meaningless words. However, for the warrior, core values such as honor, courage, loyalty, and selfless service resonate deeply within. Because of that,

The Warrior and His Core Values

core values serve to build basic character; govern and refine personal and professional temperament; sustain and refresh us when we grow weary; and guide us through the fog—the difficult challenges and often unfamiliar passages—of life itself. **Finally, they serve to bond us with the leaders and warriors of the past; those who established the heritage, traditions, and values we now embrace and cherish.**

If you do not have a defined set of core values, I recommend you embrace some specific values (3 to 5) and make them your own. Saying them is different from inculcating them. Making them your own is a process of allowing them to become the guiding values of your inner being, your warrior spirit.

In closing, I will share the core values I have adopted along the way, in my personal journey. I have embraced these values and they have been given life from two main life streams. One is my Christian faith. The other was my Christian parents. My forty-one years of marriage, and my professional careers as a naval officer and a law enforcement executive have provided the avenues and crucibles for developing and refining them.

DUTY

That act or service which is due or owed. A sense of personal duty is a concept that has almost disappeared from our culture's psyche. We desperately need a sense of personal allegiance to the obligatory tasks, service

Part 4 - Warrior Leadership and Warrior Values

and function that arise from our positions in our families, in the work place, in the church, in our communities, and to each other. This is especially true for men in terms of our duty to our God, our wives, our children, our church, our neighbors, our employer, our community, and our nation. For a people to be strong and vibrant, duty must be a compelling thought in the culture and a defining quality of its leaders. For the warrior, duty provides legs on which honor and service can run.

HONOR

The esteem due or paid to worth. Individually, and as a culture we often honor amiss, which then weakens our very fabric as a people. As we purpose to embrace the tenets of our oaths (military, law enforcement, etc.), our vows and contracts (marriage, business etc,), sacred values of our faith and honored traditions of our nation and community, a natural stream bed forms for honor to flow. When we privately and publicly honor the authorities in our lives, Biblical and Constitutional, we help preserve and strengthen our culture. When we kneel to pray, salute our flag, or stand up at appropriate times to greet others we have simply done our duty to honor our God, our Nation, and others.

SERVICE

Acts or deeds rendered for the benefit of another. As noted earlier, the Army has seven core values with one

The Warrior and His Core Values

being "selfless service." This core value appears often in corporate and church listings, and is the central theme of numerous service clubs, e.g. Rotary. I have come to understand that acts of service rendered to benefit others are a fundamental duty to be rendered in every area of life. Such acts of self-abnegation are really an integral part of the process of how we advance the cause of fulfilling our purpose for living. Jesus Christ, our consummate example, who being in very nature God, humbled himself and took on the very nature of a servant. His answer to duty's call honored the desire of Father God and rendered the greatest act of service in all of history.

The true warrior spirit is governed by a sacred set of core values and you should know them as well as your own name. If you have not already done so, identify with a personal set of core values and the essential tenets and maxims that govern them. Then develop a working definition of each one for deposit in your core. Then simply ensure that they are getting exercised regularly and in a forthright manner. Carpe Diem!

> THE TRUE WARRIOR SPIRIT IS GOVERNED BY A SACRED SET OF CORE VALUES

The format of these three core values was inspired by General Douglass MacArthur's famous speech, *Duty, Honor, Country* delivered at West Point on May 12, 1962.

Part 4 - Warrior Leadership and Warrior Values

> When we privately and publicly honor the authorities in our lives, Biblical and Constitutional, we help preserve and strengthen our culture.
>
> John R. "Barney" Barnes, CDR USN Ret.

Chapter 25

CREEDS, OATHS, AND THE WARRIOR SPIRIT

"Where is the security for property, for reputation, for life, if the sense of religious obligation desert the oaths."

George Washington, Farewell Address

Recently I was reviewing some old personal files and came across *A Navy Flyer's Creed* and my original oath of office. These were elements of my commissioning ceremony as a Naval Officer on April 25, 1969. As a result, I began to think about America in 2011 and of the symbiotic relationship of personal creeds, oaths and honor to each other. These cherished codes and ideals also have *a symbiotic relationship to the strength, integrity and sovereignty of the Nation.*

A creed is defined as any system of principles that are believed or professed by an individual. In the Christian faith the Apostles' Creed and the Nicene Creed are familiar

Part 4 - Warrior Leadership and Warrior Values

terms that embody the essence of Christianity and define who Jesus Christ is. Likewise the Boy Scout Creed, that clearly and concisely defines who a "boy scout" is, would be a familiar term in many sectors of our culture. The term *scout's honor* is an accepted rubric of our modern lexicon and the term *Be Prepared* is commonly associated with Boy Scouts.

> OATH—A SOLEMN AFFIRMATION OF PROMISE ATTESTING THE TRUTH OF AND/OR LOYALTY TO A PARTICULAR SET OF PRINCIPLES.

An oath could be defined as a solemn affirmation or promise attesting to the truth of and/or loyalty to a particular set of principles. The Hippocratic Oath, which forbids euthanasia and abortion, (formerly required of all entering the medical profession) is a classic example of a personal allegiance to a specific set of principles. Likewise the solemn, sacred oath taken by those entering into offices of public trust, e.g. political, judicial, military, public safety, etc. always require an allegiance to support and defend the Constitution. There is also the specific language to be obedient and accountable, and to faithfully discharge you duties "so help me God."

Honor could then be measured in the life of a person who has identified with a particular creed and swore an

CREEDS, OATHS, AND THE WARRIOR SPIRIT

oath of loyalty to that creed. By the testimony of their life, mirrored in the tenets of the creed and the oath they swore to be governed by, a framework for the manifestation of *honor or dishonor can be established*. Needless to say, the news of the day often contains the pathetic, sometimes tragic, tales of certain officials dishonoring their sacred oaths by their careless, unfaithful and unethical conduct. Such stories tend to foster a decline in the public trust and that can weaken national life. Divorce rates are another example of a weakening social fabric.

Most military and public safety personnel can readily identify with this thought progression. Over the years I have observed a common core quality that most of these professionals have a passion to simply serve others. For them, the news of the day often contains the heroic, sometimes tragic, details of the honoring of their oaths by risking their own lives and personal safety in the service of others. *They have responded to a calling on their lives, codified by creeds and oaths*. However, their passion "to prepare themselves to protect and serve others" is the heart of the matter. Their stories tend to foster an increase in the public trust and that can strengthen national life.

Over the course of my 38 years of professional life I was always sworn by an oath of office that was *founded upon a system of principles that I believed in*. These oaths, both military and law enforcement, required a personal allegiance to uphold and defend the Constitution of the United States. Accordingly, the ultimate authority of the

Part 4 - Warrior Leadership and Warrior Values

office I occupied resided with "the people." I was always relieved that these oaths ended with the phrase *so help me God*. This was because of the sacred nature of the oath and the responsibility incumbent upon me to fulfill the serious obligations that the oath prescribed.

I was recently reviewing the various creeds and oaths listed above, as well as others, and was impressed by the clarity and profundity of each of them. The Boy Scout Creed begins simply…"To be trustworthy in all things." Wow! In a total of just 63 simple words a system of principles is succinctly proclaimed that could transform any culture where implemented. If you have never read the Boy Scout Creed or the language of the creed is bit fuzzy…it would be well worth a few moments of your time. I think most pastors would be very pleased to have a congregation full of folks who "were good scouts." Check out the Nicene Creed too!

Navy Flyer's Creed

A few phrases from *A Navy Flyer's Creed*…"I am a United States Navy flyer…My countrymen built the best airplane in the world and entrusted it to me. They trained me to fly it. I will use it to the absolute limit of my power…I will do anything necessary to carry out our tremendous responsibilities…When the going is fast and rough, I will not falter. I will be uncompromising in every blow I strike. I will be humble in victory…my countrymen and their way of life are worthy of my greatest protective effort. I ask the help of God in making that effort great enough."

Creeds, Oaths, and the Warrior Spirit

Adherence to a creed or oath that establishes the parameters for your conduct and sets the expectations of your commitment seems a bit unpopular in our culture. However, the warrior spirit welcomes the opportunity to surrender oneself to such order.

Spiritual Warrior's Creed

Now think about a similar *Spiritual Warrior's Creed* ... "I am a spiritual warrior in God's Holy Army saved by His grace...I serve an awesome God who has entrusted the Gospel to me...He has provided me with eternal salvation, the training to share it and given me the Holy Spirit's power. I will use it to the absolute limit of my authority in Him...I will do whatever is necessary to carry out my tremendous responsibilities...When the going gets fast and rough, I will not falter. I will be uncompromising in every blow I strike. I will be humble in victory. My family, my church family, my community and my countrymen and their way of life are worthy of my greatest protective effort. I ask the help of God in making that effort great enough."

Although my last carrier landing was 28 years ago, the desire to strap a navy aircraft to my back remains strong. Likewise, my retirement from law enforcement, just three years ago, did not lessen my desire to bring criminals to justice. Yes, I know, Fantasy Land is at Disney World. Nevertheless, let us do a quick reality check and *access our passion, our posture, our fighting stance* if you will, here in 2012. This is absolutely necessary because *we*

Part 4 - Warrior Leadership and Warrior Values

will either be seated as spectators over the coming months or we will be contending for victory as participants on the arena floor..."on the tip of the spear." Joshua 24:15 comes to mind.

You may or may not have had the privilege to serve under the authority of a specific creed or oath such as I have...but the issue is what now? Perhaps the slightly modified phrases in the spiritual warrior's creed above will help you focus or you may give the Boy Scout Creed a fearless review. Now that's a challenge! Of course these suggestions are not intended to set aside any biblical teachings, but perhaps they might assist you in fulfilling the Great Commandment and The Great Commission and all while preserving our dearest liberties and our way of life. Such an objective set of imperatives could even assist you in being a more effective parent or spouse, church member, neighbor, business person, and American.

> IT IS THE CHARACTER OF A BRAVE AND RESOLUTE MAN NOT TO BE RUFFLED BY ADVERSITY AND NOT TO DESERT HIS POST.
>
> —MARCUS TULLIUS CICERO
> (106 BC-43 BC)

PART FOUR

WARRIOR LEADERSHIP AND WARRIOR VALUES

Thoughts for Individual Reflection or Group Discussion

Chapter 22

1. Discuss the central leadership precept of Xenophon and of Jesus.

2. How was their expectation of followers very similar?

3. Have you ever been under a "bia" type leader, perhaps a parent?

4. From 1 Corinthians 4:16 discuss why Paul may have had such a loyal following.

Part 4—Warrior Leadership and Warrior Values

Chapter 23

1. Discuss Chabrais' quote about an army of sheep led by a lion.

2. God made the lion "king." What can we learn about man from observing the lion?

3. Comment on, "For any kingdom to survive the King must have heirs."

4. Discuss the similarity of man's role to the male lion on the savannahs of Tsavo.

Chapter 24

1. Discuss the concept of a personal set of core values.

2. Discuss the differences in core values and character.

3. Have you previously thought a lot about "your duties?" Discuss.

4. Identify your own personal core values with a working definition of each.

Chapter 25

1. Define and discuss what purpose a creed serves.

2. Define and discuss what purpose an oath serves.

3. How did the Spiritual Warrior's Creed impact you?

PART FIVE

WARFARE THEORY AND PRACTICE

Part 5—Warfare Theory and Practice

CHAPTER 26

CENTER OF GRAVITY

WHAT EVERY SPIRITUAL WARRIOR MUST UNDERSTAND

INTRODUCTION

Center of gravity is a term which has application in several realms: physics, aerodynamics, warfare, and human anatomy. It is also applicable to culture in general. When operating in these different realms an understanding of center of gravity or "CG" is useful and at times even critical.

In physics, the CG is the center point of an object's weight distribution, where the force of gravity acts or converges and the total weight of a body is concentrated. In aerodynamics CG is essential to the safety of the flight of an aircraft. Exceeding its limits has caused many crashes. The center of gravity is the point at which the aircraft would be balanced if it were suspended from that point.

In humans, CG is located behind and just below the navel. Much of the theory in martial arts is based on keeping your balance while unbalancing your opponent. In culture, CG is the point of greatest importance, interest, or activity. As an example, for centuries the CG for the English language was Great Britain. After World War II, the balance shifted to America, along with the leadership of the western world.

Regardless of the realm being discussed, CG is about balance. We will focus on the well established warfare application of CG, with a goal of determining spiritual warfare applications. Any discussion of CG and warfare will begin and end with Carl Von Clausewitz, the master Prussian military theorist, who introduced the term "center of gravity" in his 1830 classic <u>On War</u>.

Clausewitz served as Director of the War College from 1818 to 1830 and was a veteran of many classic European war campaigns. Among his opponents was Napoleon. While at the War College in Berlin he was influenced by a friend and colleague, the German physicist Paul Erman. The two professors had a cordial relationship and exchanged ideas related to the mechanical sciences as well as warfare.

Clausewitz became fascinated by his newly acquired knowledge of physics. He was particularly interested in CG in that it represented the point at which a force applied to

Center of Gravity

an object would move it most efficiently. In other words, there would be no waste of energy in moving the object. Therefore, striking at the CG with just enough force could cause an object, say an enemy army or nation, to lose its balance or equilibrium, and fall. CG therefore, is not a source of strength but a factor of balance. As Clausewitz would say, "the hub of all power and movement on which everything depends. This is the point against which all our energies should be directed."

> CG—
> THE HUB OF ALL POWER AND MOVEMENT ON WHICH EVERYTHING DEPENDS.

Many great field generals and admirals have since become serious students of Clausewitz. His many theories regarding war and strategic thinking have become integral parts of the military force doctrines of many nations, including the United States.

The essence of a plan for a military campaign is to attack the enemy's CG while protecting your own. General Norman Schwarzkopf, an ardent student of Clausewitz, used the time allotted during Desert Shield to apply this principle and identify Iraqi Centers of Gravity. He and his planners determined there were three CGs, strategic leadership, the Republican Guard, and Iraq's nuclear, chemical and biological capability.

Part 5—Warfare Theory and Practice

The rapid unbalancing of these CG's made for the speedy achievement of Kuwait's liberation. It also made for great television for American "couch warriors." Another example can be noted in The War Between the States. The Confederate Army of Northern Virginia was a CG for much of the South's effort. For a time, it prevented the Federal Army of the Potomac from capturing Richmond. However, once this CG was struck with the proper force, total victory came quickly.

Spiritual Application

The current official Department of Defense definition of Center of Gravity is "those characteristics, capabilities, or localities from which a military force derives its freedom of action, physical strength, or will to fight." Knowing what you now know about CG, can Centers of Gravity within the local church, denominations, or the Kingdom generally be identified? If so, would that be prudent or relevant? It seems to me that the forces of darkness, which we face daily, are themselves aware of the concept of CG and have executed plans to deliver force against spiritual CGs whether we acknowledge the fact or not.

This gives credence to the targeting of leadership in the spiritual kingdom. Taking out the five-fold ministry creates a vacuum in leadership that leaves the church in utter disarray. This is true, simply because of their critical role in building and strengthening the church and related spiritual kingdom. (See Ephesians 4:11-13). No wonder

Christian leaders are such major objectives and are identified as target CGs.

When Japan overran Korea in 1905, one of their strategies was to kill or imprison pastors and leaders among other religions, an example of an enemy identifying a CG. This same scenario has unfolded numerous times in history, even into the 21st Century. In this case, one of the provocations was Korea's unwillingness to bear allegiance to the Emperor, whom the Japanese worshipped as a God. This is but one example of Satan's awareness and use of temporal power to impact a spiritual CG. According to testimony from Dr. David Yonggi Cho, the church in Korea suffered greatly because of the decentralizing of authority and chaos it created.

Spiritual truths are another CG under attack. Doing so leaves Christians confused about what is and what is not believable. In such a condition, some are left with non-biblical or anti-biblical assumptions, such as "Islam and Christianity serve the same God" and "all religions lead to the same place," etc.

Perhaps the term "strategic entity" will be helpful in expanding this point. In warfare planning, a strategic entity has five component rings, or CGs, of concentric circles: Leadership, organic essentials (administrative organization, etc), infrastructure, population, and fielded forces. This was mentioned earlier in referring to the Gulf War. It is relatively easy to imagine these concentric circles in an overlay grid of an established denomination,

Part 5—Warfare Theory and Practice

a growing and prospering church in a municipality, or even a para-church organization.

As an example, for instructional purposes only, let us say we are war planners and have been assigned to develop a plan to take down Iran. First we would identify the strategic leadership and fielded forces, making sure that we understood the concentric circle relationship. Then our plan would be to strike these CGs violently and in parallel. Next, we would evaluate the three remaining strategic entities, (something we should have done earlier in Iraq,) to see if they remained as viable CGs. In the spiritual realm of evil, the planning grid for attacking the Church would likely be Christian leaders on various levels, followed by other identified strategic entities in concentric rings. It would really have been awesome to get C. S. Lewis' take on the whole concept of spiritual CG.

Perhaps some other spiritual strategic entities would be influential Christians in secular leadership positions, pastors in general, and praise and worship leaders. Finally, the enemy would likely identify the "fielded forces" associated with those entities. These would be that 10% to 15% of believers who are actual threats to the kingdom of darkness.

Sheep scatter easily without shepherds (population) and buildings (infrastructure.)They become confused and disoriented without administrative organization (organic essentials). These are not generally a major threat to Satan's plans. In fact, I believe the demonic forces arrayed

Center of Gravity

against the American Church are pleased that we contain so much of our activity within our buildings. However consider this; an effective campaign against the Church in China would be much more difficult and complex. (Just ask the Communist government) Ponder that for a moment!

A center of gravity is always found where the mass is most densely concentrated. This makes it the most vulnerable target, and the most effective place to strike with force. There is a very familiar Scripture passage which describes the principle of CG perfectly. In Matthew 4:1-11, Jesus has been led by the Holy Spirit into a place of fasting and isolation. After forty days He is tempted by Satan. It is interesting that Clausewitz described the clash of armies or collision of CGs as *much like two wrestlers grappling*, each trying to unbalance and pin the other.

In the wilderness, a similar clash happened in the spiritual realm. I believe this event should be instructive for the conduct of all Believers when encountering demonic forces. If you are familiar with Bruce Lee or Chuck Norris it will be helpful if you would picture one of their classic bouts with the #1 evil character. Satan employed his basic weapon system, deception, first used against Eve in Genesis. Satan, as we know,

Part 5—Warfare Theory and Practice

actually is the father of lies and a major twister of truth. (See John 8:44).

Satan, knowing Jesus was in human form, targeted the three major chinks in man's armor; the lust of the flesh, the lust of the eyes, and pride of life. Jesus, on the other hand, *was led by the Spirit*. That, we know, is always the best model. He simply countered each blow of Satan with Truth! (See 1 John 3:8). I like to think of this spiritual bout in this manner. Jesus let Satan "throw the first blow," striking at His weak and hungry state. So Satan was taken "off balance", much like a martial arts technique of Bruce Lee or Chuck Norris.

Then Jesus countered with His primary weapon of Truth, Deuteronomy 8:3, striking Satan's CG of "liar." Then it is Satan's move who strikes at pride, and at the temple in Jerusalem of all places. Ponder that a moment. Satan also backs his move up with Psalms 91:11-12. Wow! Jesus simply counters with Truth, Deuteronomy 6:16, striking another blow to Satan's CG of lies and twisted truth. At last Satan goes for all the marbles with a visual offering of all the kingdoms of the earth, *"if You will fall down and worship me."* Jesus, again giving us a pattern for spiritual warfare, strikes an artful blow to Satan's CG of "deceiver." The bout-ending-blow of Truth was Deuteronomy 6:13. This was like a spiritual "round house kick" to the head. This should give you a better appreciation of Deuteronomy— "The Gospel of Moses."

Jesus being tempted by Satan is a familiar account to most Christians, but think of it now in "Clausewitzian" terms. Satan came directly at the CG, i.e. those characteristics and capabilities from which a force derives its freedom of action, strength, and will to fight, and those vulnerabilities which would have unbalanced his opponent. Although Satan "went for the kill", true statements laced with deception proved totally ineffective and were summarily dispatched. Jesus, though weakened physically, responded skillfully with simple Truth directed to the hub (CG) of the power on which everything in Satan's plan depended. Jesus, the consummate leader and warrior, perfectly demonstrated how we are to deal with evil spiritual forces.

A Spiritual/Natural Warfare Dynamic?

We are often reminded in Scripture, such as in 2 Corinthians 10:3-5, that victory against evil spiritual forces is not a matter of physical strength or intellectual prowess. In matters of spiritual warfare my experience has been that Christians tend to quickly arrive at Ephesians 6:11-20, ready to charge into the battle, without passing thru Ephesians 1:1 to 6:10!

During the Vietnam War, I flew over 500 combat missions, almost always, clad in combat gear from head to toe. A couple of times there was not enough time to grab everything. My point is that there were twenty-two months of intense internalized training, including two months of actual combat that were necessary to prepare

Part 5—Warfare Theory and Practice

me to be an "effective" combat aviator. Anyone can suit up on game day...but then what?

In Romans 13:12, Paul exhorts us to *put aside the deeds of darkness and put on the armor of light.* This principle, stated in other passages as well, is what changes our individual CG from the natural or carnal one (behind and below the navel) to a spiritual one, located in our inner most being. This puts the spiritual warrior in an alert fighting stance, on our toes, and prevents being knocked "off our feet" by a perversion of one of our five senses, or the compromise of deception by half truths.

> PAUL EXORTS US TO PUT ASIDE THE DEEDS OF DARKNESS AND PUT ON THE ARMOR OF LIGHT.

As uncompromised Truth is proclaimed by leaders and affirmed by all believers, then the slightly twisted truth and outright deceptions we encounter will be knocked off balance. Local church bodies will then be strengthened and the "fielded forces" will be greatly increased in our congregations (populations). Ephesians 4:15 will become the norm rather than wishful thinking.

John 16:13 describes an immovable CG that no force can budge or unbalance. It is so simple yet so profound that it can be missed in our many books, videos, and seminars. As we build our individual lives, families, and church body on the *Chief Cornerstone and the foundation of the apostles and prophets.* (See Ephesians 2:20-22), we build on the Truth and with the Truth. The result is that the Kingdom of God is manifest.

The first century Church did just that and became a CG, which unbalanced the three opposing CGs of Greek culture, Jewish religion, and finally the Roman Empire. In fact, the Roman Emperor Constantine became the first Christian Emperor on October 29, 312 just after the greatest Christian persecutions under Emperors Diocletian and Galerius had ended.

Both incredible and miraculous, Constantine, though out numbered 2 or 3 to 1, had defeated several Roman armies on his march south to Rome. According to Eusebius (220-329), the Bishop of Caesarea, Constantine and his whole army, while on the march, had seen a vision of a cross in the sky at about noon. Constantine described the vision as "a trophy of the cross of light in the heavens, above the sun, and bearing the inscription *In Hoc Signo Vinces* or In This Sign You Will Conquer."

Prior to the crucial battle with the Imperial Roman army guarding Rome, on 28 October, 312 Constantine had the cross symbol he had seen in the vision placed on the shields and armaments of his soldiers. Though outnumbered over 2 to 1, Constantine, with the first army officially identified as "Christian" quickly routed and destroyed the army of Maxientius. This very brief battle altered the natural CG of the western world for many generations, demonstrating the effectiveness of spiritual warfare and the fervent prayer of Christians in that era.

Final Thoughts

Jesus demonstrated, for both temporal and spiritual powers, the reality of "the hub of all power and movement on which everything depends…the point at which all our energies should be directed." Jesus revealed for all history the ultimate center of gravity that no power can push off balance, Truth!

Although still in human form Jesus neither needed nor used his physical strength in this spiritual demonstration of "ultimate extreme fighting." The wilderness encounter with Satan was epic and monumental, giving followers of Christ a basic template with which to operate against demonic forces during this or any age.

The great warrior, King David, came to understand CG very well in both natural and spiritual warfare. The wheels really do come off of our best chariots and our strongest and fastest horses occasionally become lame. I say this is in reference to some of our many church programs. In modern America it would be well to remember David's thoughts on this subject. *Some trust in chariots and some in horses, but we trust in the name of the Lord our God* Psalm 20:7 (NIV).

CHAPTER 27

THE NINE PRINCIPLES OF WAR

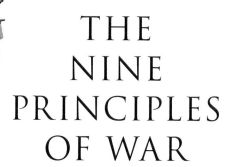

In the natural order I belong to *the warrior class* as a cultural fact distinctly separated from the academic, business, financial, technological, and other major cultural divisions. Although I may venture into these other divisions from time to time my desire, *my longing is to be among warriors.* My position in the warrior class is somewhat established by virtue of my professional training and serving 24 years as a Naval Officer, flying 507 combat missions with the elite Navy Seawolves, working closely with navy SEALs in combat, commanding a South Carolina State Guard Battalion for two years, and serving 12 years on the command staff of a local sheriff's office.

However, for purposes of this discussion, I must emphasize the fact that some of the most exemplary "warriors" I have known have been civilian as well as

Part 5—Warrior Theory and Practice

military and both martial and spiritual. For many years I have considered myself to also be a spiritual warrior and as such have often engaged in what I understood to be spiritual warfare. This would include such pursuits as; a weekly church prayer meeting; prayer meetings in my home; Christian military or law enforcement personnel meeting together to pray; meeting with civic leaders to pray; and then taking action in those arenas to push against the darkness and establish righteousness in the realms I operated in.

Christian leaders of all stripes often speak of "fighting the enemy" or teaching from Ephesians 6:10-17 about the whole armor of God as "spiritual warfare" or perhaps 2 Corinthians 10:4-9 which clarifies that we have "mighty" spiritual weaponry for the purpose of defeating evil. We are also familiar with the numerous Old Testament accounts of actual warfare and the concept of natural Israel and spiritual Israel.

As a member of the profession of arms I have often been curious about such subjects as measuring the effectiveness of specific prayer efforts. For instance, let us say that a church or several churches engaged in "spiritual warfare" over a part of town in somewhat of a coordinated manner for 12 months. Let us also say that intercessors are deeply involved and that all the appropriate spiritual authorities are giving leadership to the effort. If we began this prayer campaign on 1 January we should be able to see some evidence of increased righteousness by the following 1 January. Lower crime rates, lower suicide rates, increased fervor among church members, increased attendance or increased giving would seem to be reasonable evidences of a weakened enemy. A shorter term campaign would be Daniel's 21 day experience battling with the "Prince" over Persia.

A warrior spirit, like in Daniel, is essential for victory on the natural and spiritual battlefields of life. By warrior spirit I mean *the passionate desire and determination in the heart of a man, a desire to perfect oneself for the service to others.* Daniel, as we well know, faithfully served his people, a sequence of kings and his God with courage and integrity. Daniel was infused with the same warrior spirit as was Joshua and Gideon.

> AMERICAN CULTURE OFTEN CONTRADICTS GOD'S PLAN FOR BOYS TO BECOME MEN.

Knowing that satanic forces have plans, it would seem to me that Christians should have principled war plan strategies that match their rhetoric to counter these evil forces in the realm of spiritual warfare. It is for this reason that I offer the following discussion on *The Nine Principles of War.*

HISTORICAL PERSPECTIVE

In all of the nations of the world that have military academies, the subject of *principles of war* occupies an

Part 5—Warrior Theory and Practice

integral part of doctrinal instruction. Accordingly, each of the United States military academies, all of our war colleges, and all of our combat arms schools feature instruction on the subject of *principles of war*. In the United States military *nine principles* are emphasized which are considered the foremost and cardinal precepts and concepts which, if followed, will enable one force to face and defeat another force.

These nine principles primarily come to us from Baron Carl Von Clausewitz, the great Prussian soldier, military thinker and strategist. Clausewitz published his classic *On War* in 1830 and it has been studied and implemented by most great military leaders around the globe from 1830 to the present day. The exhaustive material in *On War* is extracted from historical militarist and in various subject areas to instruct warriors how to direct their tactical thinking when planning for a single battle or for a broader strategic war plan. A significant area of this study is what is commonly referred to as *The Nine Principles of War*.

I am somewhat of a student of military history which includes a study of history's great wars and the battles that comprised them. What I have observed is that these nine principles have been in play throughout history and have in fact proven to be both cardinal and ageless in determining the outcomes of thousands of land and naval battles.

A classic example of *the nine principles in action* would be the Battle of Cannae. Fought on August 2, 214 BC, it is

The Nine Principles of War

one of the greatest tactical victories in military history. During the Second Punic War, the great Carthaginian General Hannibal, with an allied army of 54,000 troops, defeated a force of 16 Roman and allied legions (87,000 troops) led by consuls Lucius Paullus and Gaius Varro. In this very decisive and consequential battle it is a most astonishing fact that 60,000 Roman and allied troops were killed while Hannibal only suffered the loss of 6000. In addition to these factors Cannae is south of Rome, sort of "home turf," which makes the outcome even more remarkable.

In studying the Battle of Cannae, I can not find even one the *nine principles* that were followed by Gaius Varro, perhaps others can. On the other hand, Hannibal carefully employed several of them. This is a fascinating battle and can be easily reviewed on line to any degree desired. For instance, Paullo was very cautious and deliberative whereas Varro was reckless and overconfident. This human factor, combined with the fact that Roman law required that they alternate their command on a daily basis, contributed significantly to the outcome. Hannibal, who was well aware of these human factors, exploited them with surgical precision luring the Romans to attack at a time of Hannibal's choosing, on a day that Gaius Varro was in command.

In the next section we will review these nine principles while pursuing the premise that they can apply to spiritual warfare. By so doing I believe we can, in various degrees, improve our *spiritual battlefield effectiveness?*

Part 5—Warrior Theory and Practice

THE NINE PRINCIPLES

1. OBJECTIVE:

Every military operation, especially in wartime, should be directed towards a defined and attainable objective. Every initiative must be directed towards crushing the enemy's capacity to fight. The Vietnam War, in which I fought, is a classic illustration of the folly of ignoring this principle. Clear objectives, beyond fighting and killing the enemy we were facing each night and day and propping up an anemic South Vietnamese government, became blurred as months turned into years. American forces consistently prevailed in battle against a significantly numerically superior enemy force. However, objectives became more elusive as politicians increasingly tinkered with the battlefield.

Conversely the First Gulf War, led by General Norman Schwarzkopf, is a classic example of following this principle. One well defined objective ruled the day--- "free the Nation of Kuwait from the occupying Iraqi Army." Accordingly, the military power of the nation was focused on this one clear objective that was announced to the entire world. All military personnel, from generals to privates, knew what we were about to do. Saddam Hussein also knew!

2. OFFENSIVE:

Seize, retain, and exploit the initiative. Victory is unattainable while "hunkered down" with a defensive

The Nine Principles of War

mentality. General George S. Patton led the 3rd Army sweeping across Europe in the Summer of 1944 and by late Winter of 1945 had gone farther faster, conquered more territory, and had killed, wounded and captured more enemy soldiers than any army in the history of war. General Patton would say **"In war, the only sure defense is offense,** and the efficiency of the offense depends upon the warlike souls of those conducting it...wars are not won with defensive tactics...wars are lost in the mind before they are lost on the ground...we must have a superiority complex...Always attack."

3. MASS:

Apply sufficient force to achieve the objective at the decisive place and time. Mass does not necessarily mean "more troops" such as General Picket's Charge where he led 12,500 men during the *Battle of Gettysburg* on July 3, 1863. In fact this tactical blunder by General Robert E. Lee not only lost the battle but needlessly maimed and killed thousands of men. Certainly a modern example of this principle is the term *shock and awe* employed in the routing and defeating of the Iraqi Army under Saddam Hussein. In a more comprehensive context, the German armies of WW2 used the term *blitzkrieg* as they rapidly ran across entire nations beginning with Poland on September 1, 1939. The German army employed all nine principles often and with perfection.

4. ECONOMY OF FORCE:

Focus the right amount of force on the key objective and, equally important, do not waste precious resources

Part 5—Warrior Theory and Practice

and force on secondary objectives. The infamous *Black Hawk Down* incident in Somalia in 1993 is an example of the results of ignoring this principle. The "right amount" of force was available, however political tinkering rather than principled military doctrine was employed. The tragic result was the needless loss of 19 brave warriors, two aircraft, and national honor.

A classic example of this principle in action is the famous *Raid on Entebbe* on July 4, 1976 in which the Israeli Army rescued 260 hostages being held in Uganda. This audacious and daring raid, like all successful operations, employed several principles but showcased *economy of force* on a key objective.

5. MANEUVER:

Place the enemy in a position of disadvantage through the flexible application of combat power. Maneuver in of itself can produce no decisive results, but can make decisive results possible. During The War Between The States, General Thomas J. "Stonewall" Jackson became legendary for his employment of this principle particularly in what is known as *The Valley Campaign*.

During the spring of 1862 he led 17,000 men with audacity over 648 miles in 48 days to win five significant battles over a combined Union force of 60,000 in the Shenandoah Valley. His main objective was to prevent these forces from uniting with other forces in a siege of Richmond. The Valley Campaign was largely a great success and denied Union forces a *principled* response.

The Nine Principles of War

6. UNITY OF COMMAND:

For every objective there must be a unified effort and one person responsible for command decisions that must not be impeded by politics and "second guessing." One of the best examples of this principle occurred on June 6, 1944 with *D-Day* and the allied invasion of Europe. General Dwight D. Eisenhower was The Supreme Allied Commander. He had cancelled the invasion earlier due to the weather, however, on June 6 with the weather still a bit marginal, he alone made the decision to launch the largest invasion in human history. It is of interest to note that General Eisenhower had prepared statements for both the success and the failure of the invasion. For success he credited the bravery and sacrifice of the soldiers, sailors and marines...for failure he accepted full and personal responsibility.

7. SECURITY:

Never permit the enemy to acquire an unexpected or unpredicted advantage. Take all measures, including detailed planning, to avoid "surprise." Napoleon Bonaparte was one of the greatest generals in history but had this to say about himself: "It is not genius which reveals to me suddenly and secretly what I should do in circumstances unexpected by others, it is thought and preparation."

Certainly one of the more memorable examples of the importance of this principle was the events surrounding the Japanese attack upon Pearl Harbor on December

Part 5—Warrior Theory and Practice

7, 1941. Our failure to carefully embrace this principle cost us dearly then and was in play to some degree on September 11, 2001. "The price of freedom is eternal vigilance" (Thomas Jefferson).

8. SURPRISE:

Strike the enemy at a time and/or place and in a manner for which he is unprepared. Perhaps one of the best examples of this principle was demonstrated at the great naval *Battle of Trafalgar* on October 21, 1805. British Admiral Horatio Nelson, with 17,000 men and 27 ships of the line were sailing against a combined French and Spanish force of 30,000 men and 33 ships of the line. Admiral Nelson had briefed his captains over "two evening meals" that they would attack with *a surprise tactic*. Rather that seek to slug it out in conventional broadside engagements, Nelson directed the smaller, faster British ships to line up single file in two separate formations.

Admiral Nelson led one formation sailing eastward while Collingwood led the second formation, parallel of Nelson to the south, as they both sailed directly into the enemy armada sailing north. This attack was bold, daring and a total surprise.

Although Nelson died from wounds in the battle, he lived to see the outcome. The British losses were 449 killed none captured and no ships lost whereas the French/Spanish losses were 4,480 killed, 7000 captured, and 22 ships lost. Nelson's audacity on one afternoon changed the history of Europe for 100 years.

The Nine Principles of War

9. SIMPLICITY:

Prepare clear, uncomplicated plans and clear concise orders. Always ensure a thorough understanding by all involved. Simplicity must allow for flexibility to adjust to changing conditions, recognize the training level and skills of those engaged, and audacity at engaging targets of opportunity. Modern "special warfare" warriors such as Navy SEALs, Army Green Berets, Delta Force and others often operate with very complex and sophisticated equipment. However, their successes are legendary because they adhere to principles of war often emphasizing "simplicity." "Success in war depends upon the golden rule of war—Speed—Simplicity—Boldness" General George S. Patton

APPLICATION TO SPIRITUAL WARFARE

As we have reviewed each of the nine principles, with a brief example of their historical application in actual battles, you may have had some thoughts on a practical application of at least some of the principles in spiritual warfare. You may have remembered some watershed experience in a corporate prayer initiative where the principles were in play. Perhaps you were able to identify with one of these principles in a successful or failed initiative with which you were a part of.

Well known events, such as the fall of The Soviet Union, are believed by many to be a witness for concentrated and

Part 5—Warrior Theory and Practice

focused prayer being the catalyst for the sweeping and monumental political change. At that time, 1991, there were many such testimonies coming out of Germany, Poland, Czechoslovakia, Romania, and other countries as to the paramount importance of prayer. *With hindsight, we can see how this historical example of spiritual warfare featured such principles as objective, unity, offensive, simplicity, and mass.*

As we look at our world today and the communities in which we live and work, it is obvious that we have much to do. In my view prayer (spiritual warfare) is often misused, misunderstood or even neglected. Principled spiritual warfare must be incorporated effectively into a local effort to subdue and defeat the very formidable and evil spiritual forces arrayed against the local Church.

When you think about it, all battles are local events where opposing forces clash and with one most likely an invader. This begs the question for every locale, *"is the church the occupying force or the invader?"* Whichever the case and it will vary, unified *local spiritual warfare* initiatives against a common enemy are of greater importance today than many have thought! Corporate prayer meetings, if they occur at all, are often the least attended meetings in the life of the church, especially by men. Strategic planning is most often centered on budgets and "flock maintenance" rather than spiritual warfare planning and Kingdom expansion. The result is that *many churches operate more like a field hospital than a healthy fighting unit.*

The Nine Principles of War

Combined prayer initiatives by even two congregations are almost non-existent. I believe that effective prayer is much like the "air war" which often precedes the "ground war" in modern warfare or say a robust naval bombardment prior to an invasion. In both cases the enemy is weakened and friendly casualties are reduced.

My experience has taught me that it is a daunting task to bring pastors together for meaningful councils of spiritual warfare. Most will respond with something along the line of "well, let's just get everybody praying (in their building) and we will be just fine." *In the absence of spiritual generalship in a city or even a section of town these nine principles will generally lie dormant and untested in real spiritual warfare.*

Please allow me to challenge you with some basic questions. Do you think that coordinated spiritual warfare, let us say in a local community, even a multi-county area or larger area, may have significant degrees of effectiveness?

Could the *Nine Principles of War*, if known and studied possibly improve our *spiritual battlefield effectiveness?* Could

COULD SUCH UNIFIED, STRATEGIC PRAYER REDUCE VIOLENCE AND EVIL ACTS SUCH AS WE OFTEN IDENTIFY AS A "CRIME RATE" IN A PARTICULAR AREA?

Part 5—Warrior Theory and Practice

such united, strategic prayer reduce violence and evil acts such as we often identify as a "crime rate" in a particular area? Lastly, do you think that some or all of these nine principles could have a place in your local church or personal prayer and spiritual warfare initiatives?

If so, why not do something unprecedented like Hannibal or Admiral Nelson! Let's be bold like those Israelis who on July 4, 1976 went deep into enemy territory, well prepared, confident and determined to free those who had been taken captive. That whole scenario reminds me of Abram's raid into enemy territory to rescue several kinsmen, including his nephew, who had been taken captive.

Genesis 14 gives us an account, and possible pattern, where several of the Nine Principles of War were employed with great success. Abram armed and led 318 "trained" men of his household about 90 miles (check your map) in pursuit of these "terrorists." The Hebrew word *chaniyk* is translated "trained" and also carries the meaning "initiated and practiced." For a warrior that would have been an exciting, challenging and "fun" mission to go on.

Genesis 14:14 tells us that Abram divided his forces "by night," which from personal experience can be a bit of a challenge. He then ordered an attack, routed, and pursued these enemies some distance. What do you think was the likelihood that these guys wanted to mess with Abram's "stuff" again? Abram, just like his descendants did at Entebbe, Uganda, rescued every single person and possession and took them home! And by so doing, Abram and his 318 warriors were the first to "own the night."

In recent days some have proffered that America is on the front end of a Third Great Awakening. If that is to be, and I pray it is, then it must be under girded with prayer and the bold exploits of spiritual warriors. Let us be those of whom others will say—they truly changed history, that they did great exploits for their God, that they brought the peace of Christ in astonishing ways into the hearts of many, that they caused great harm to Satan's forces wherever and whenever they went. *Let us not just be some obscure, ineffective and timid souls who will soon be forgotten, leaving no lasting legacy or memory that we had even lived.*

Part 5—Warrior Theory and Practice

Chapter 28

WAR CRIES AND SHOUTS

Exploring the Spiritual Application

The Lord will march out like a mighty man, like a warrior he will stir up his zeal; with a shout he will raise the battle cry and will triumph over his enemies.
Isaiah 42:13 (NIV)

The priests blew the trumpets. When the people heard the blast of the trumpets they gave a thunderclap shout. The wall fell at once. The people rushed straight into the city and took it.
Joshua 6:20 (The Message)

Some years ago I began to discover that war cries and shouts could be weapons in the arsenal of the spiritual warrior. Paul reminds us in 2 Corinthians 10:4 that the

PART 5—WARFARE THEORY AND PRACTICE

weapons of our warfare, though not the world's weapons, have the Divine power to demolish spiritual strongholds. I believe that important components in this arsenal are the war cries and shouts by the spiritual warrior. This seems not to be widely understood. Therefore it is not as effective as it could be in taming the fury of the demonic forces arrayed against the Church.

War cries—battle cries or shouts have been used throughout history by military units when facing opposing hostile units. Battle cries often evoke patriotic or religious fervor such as *Allahu Akbar* (God is great) used by Muslim armies for centuries. This continues to be a battle cry for many modern Muslim armies such as Pakistan. All too well, we know it is also used by Islamic Jihadists immediately preceding a terror attack.

With great emotion, ancient Greek warriors, Spartans and Athenians, charged into battle shouting patriotic chants such as *alala,* which was supposed to emulate the sound of the owl, the bird of their patron goddess Athena. *Sieg Heil,* which means Hail Victory in German, is a more modern battle cry used by the Nazi regime. Although it had been in use by the German army for many years, it has been banned since the German defeat in World War II. It is illegal to say *sieg heil* in public.

In the Middle Ages, battle cries began to appear on standards, such as *Dieu et mon droit* (God and my right), the battle cry used by English kings, like Edward III's troops during the great victory at Crecy in August, 1346.

War Cries and Shouts

At the Battle of Hastings, 1066, the Saxons used the battle cry: *Godamite!* (God Almighty), whereas the victorious Normans had the battle cry of *Dex* Aie (God aid us).

The modern word "slogan" comes to us from the Scottish-Gaelic word *slughorn,* meaning gathering cry or battle cry. Today slogans are one of the major weapons used in the corporate warfare battles. The movie <u>Brave Heart</u> depicts many dramatic moments of *slughorn,* powerfully enunciated by Mel Gibson as he portrayed William Wallace.

Battle cries have the dual effect of uniting and emboldening an army into one force, while striking fear and terror into the opposing hostile force. Witness the familiar example of the Rebel Yell, which became a hallmark of the War Between the States. A former Union soldier describes it like this. "A peculiar corkscrew sensation that went up your spine when you heard it... if you claim you heard it and weren't scared, that means you never heard it."

> BATTLE CRIES HAVE THE DUAL EFFECT OF EMBOLDENING AND UNITING AN ARMY INTO ONE FORCE

Colonel Keller Anderson of Kentucky very artfully described the Rebel Yell. "Then arose that do-or-die expression, that maniacal maelstrom of sound; that

Part 5—Warfare Theory and practice

penetrating, shrieking, rasping, blood-curdling noise that could be heard for miles and whose volume reached the heavens—such an expression as never came from the throats of sane men, but from men who the seething blast of an imaginary hell would not check while the sound lasted."

Contemporary battle cries continue to be used, although the modern battlefield often precludes their widespread usage. War cries continue to be a source of motivation and unit cohesion, especially among ground units and special warfare warriors. The U.S. Marines use the term *Oo-rah!* which is similar, but of different origin to the Russian army's *Ourrah!* and *Ura!* The U.S. Army has a similar but distinctive shout, *Hooah!* The war cry dearest to my heart is another similar but distinctive shout. *Hoo-Yah!* The battle cry of the U.S. Navy, and of course, of Navy SEALs.

The Israeli Defense Force (IDF) has a long and storied employment of battle cries and shouts that are drawn from Scripture. However the current official battle cries are *Kadima!* or "Forward!" and *Akharai!* or "After Me!" You may recall that Kadima is also one of the two major political parties in Israel, formed by the great warrior General Ariel Sharon. The Givati Brigade is an Israeli Special Forces unit having the battle cry of *Iti!* or "With Me!" and their motto is "Any Time, Any Place, Any Mission."

It seems to me that Joshua and Caleb would have been right at home in the Givati Brigade. "Iti!" In Scripture, the battle cry played an important role in the outcome of key battles. And the war cry could be mixed with the blasts of trumpets and other sounds. One obvious example is Gideon's army. In a well-coordinated night attack with 300 warriors divided into three units, the war cry was a mighty weapon. In Judges 7:20 we find Gideon launching his attack at the beginning of the mid-watch with a blast of trumpets, a breaking of jars and a *qara*, (to encounter in a hostile manner and call out to), "The sword for the Lord and of Gideon!" Then, in Joshua 6:5 we discover two distinct variations of "warfare sound.." First there is *truwah*, the seven trumpet blasts on *shofar* (ram's horns) that signal the *ruwa* (ear splitting cries aloud of triumph with trumpet blasts). It was a Divinely choreographed, perfectly executed triumph.

Still another example of "word power" is in Isaiah 42:10-14. There is singing, *shuwr* (vs. 10 singing while strolling or walking) a powerful picture of spiritual warfare, with *tsavach* (to screech exultingly vs. 11). The imagery of verse 13 should inspire and motivate the most indifferent of spiritual warriors.

> The Lord will march out like a mighty man, like a warrior he will stir up his zeal; with a shout he will raise the battle cry and will triumph over his enemies.

Finally, we turn to another familiar passage, which gives us even more insight. In Psalm 47:1 the word for shout is *ruwa*, as in Joshua 6:5;10;20. Then, in Psalm 47:5

PART 5—WARFARE THEORY AND PRACTICE

truwah is translated shout. King Jehoshaphat faced three hostile armies with a choir and *rinnah* (singing, creaking shrill sound of joy, gladness, proclamation, shouting and triumph) that brought utter confusion and routed their enemies. Evidently God enjoys our loud voices. *Shout unto God with a voice of triumph.* God is saying to get off the couch and get into the fray. There is a call to warriors, a call for Holy warriors to awaken! Lift your voices and shout unto God with a voice of triumph! Strike fear into the camp of the enemy!

> THERE IS A CALL TO WARRIORS, A CALL FOR HOLY WARRIORS TO AWAKEN.

Some leaders communicate that we are experiencing the beginnings of a 3rd Great Awakening, and I do see signs of that. The first two each spanned decades before they lost their momentum. Our duty, to influence and change the culture around us, will require some significant changes in the American Church. There are so many walls that divide us, and they must come down. Perhaps some *truwah* and *ruwa* will be in play as in the days of Joshua to take down some of these walls and barriers. Hoo-Yah!

PART FIVE

WARFARE THEORY AND PRACTICE

Thoughts for Individual Reflection or Group Discussion

Chapter 26

1. Define Center of Gravity and discuss why it is important

2. Discuss Jesus' encounter with Satan in the wilderness in terms of CG

3. Discuss strategic entity and list the five concentric rings.

4. Draw a spiritual strategic entity with the five concentric rings

PART 5—WARFARE THEORY AND PRACTICE

CHAPTER 27

1. List and discuss the nine principles

2. Discuss Clausewitz in terms of: is there a spiritual warfare application?

3. How could you apply one or more of the nine principles at work, at home, at church?

CHAPTER 28

1. Discuss your previous exposure to "war cries and shouts."

2. Did you know the origin of "slogan?" Discuss the spiritual application.

3. Discuss the spiritual "acoustics" employed in Joshua 6:5 and Judges 7:20.

4. Discuss how the war cry and the shout can be used today in spiritual warfare.

Note: There are no questions for Chapters 29-30.

PART SIX

SONGS OF WAR AND THE WARRIOR'S PRAYER

Part 6—Songs of War and The Warrior's Prayer

> Let the high praises of God be in their mouth, and a two-edged sword in their hand...To bind their kings with chains, and their nobles with fetters of iron... this honor have all His saints.
>
> –Psalm 149:6, 8, 9b (NKJV)

CHAPTER 29

ONWARD CHRISTIAN SOLDIERS

The Warrior Spirit and the Songs of War

> ...Jehoshaphat appointed men
> to sing to the Lord and to praise Him
> for the splendor of his holiness
> as they went out
> at the head of the army, saying:
> 'Give thanks to the Lord,
> for His love endures forever.
> 2 Chronicles 20:21 (NIV)

Throughout history triumphant, inspiring music and song has been an integral part of the art of war. Countless armies, while on the march and while encamped, have sung lyrics that spoke of past triumphs,

Part 6—Songs of War and The Warrior's Prayer

of cherished values and of the anticipation of future glory. For the Christian warrior, I can think of no song that better captures these themes than *Onward, Christian Soldiers*.

Although many men may be familiar with this classic hymn, they may not be familiar with its origins. The song was originally composed in 1865 by a newly arrived, 30 year-old Anglican curate, Sabine Baring-Gould, at his parish in England. An annual procession was about to take place in which Sunday school children would walk from one village to the next. The entire lyrics were written one evening solely as a marching tune for these children, with the hope it would keep them headed in the same direction, physically and spiritually.

Seventy six years later in 1941, Winston Churchill and Franklin D. Roosevelt met in a council of war to agree upon the *Atlantic Charter*. The meeting took place on the battleship *HMS Prince of Wales* during which time there was a special church service scheduled. Prime Minister Churchill and President Roosevelt were asked to choose hymns for this service and Churchill chose *Onward, Christian Soldiers*.

Later in a radio broadcast to the nation Churchill said this: "We sang *Onward, Christian Soldiers* indeed, and I felt this was no vain presumption, but that we had the right to feel that we were serving a cause for the sake of which a trumpet has sounded from on high. When I looked upon that densely packed congregation of fighting men of the same language, of the same faith, of the same fundamental laws, of the same ideals…it swept across me that here was the only hope, but also the sure hope of saving the world from measureless degradation."

Now, some 70 years later, nothing really significant seems to have changed in our world. The fact that remains is this, that the only "sure hope of saving the world from meaningless degradation" is "packed congregations of fighting men"…congregations of Christian warriors, *marching as to war, with the cross of Jesus going on before!*

The only sure hope of saving the world from meaningless degradation… is packed congregations of Christian warriors…

As I read the verses to this epic march, I feel drawn and even compelled to sing along slowly, to let each powerful word and concept resonate in my spirit. I need to close my eyes and picture that "packed congregation of fighting men" on board that British man of war, to see the resolve in their eyes, to sense their unity of spirit, to experience the vibrancy of their faith, and to share the growing anticipation of their fast approaching date with destiny.

Part 6—Songs of War and The Warrior's Prayer

Onward, Christian Soldiers

Onward, Christian soldiers, Marching as to war, With the cross of Jesus going on before!

Christ, the royal master, Leads against the foe; Forward into battle, See his banner go!

(chorus) Onward, Christian soldiers, marching as to war, with the cross of Jesus going on before.

At the sign of triumph Satan's hosts doth flee; On, then, Christian soldiers, On to victory!

Hell's foundation's quiver At the shout of praise; Brothers, lift your voices, Loud your anthems raise!

(chorus) Onward, Christian soldiers, marching as to war, with the cross of Jesus going on before.

Like a mighty army Moves the church of God; Brothers, we are treading Where the saints have trod; We are not divided; All one body we, One in hope and doctrine, One in Charity.

(chorus) Onward, Christian soldiers, marching as to war, with the cross of Jesus going on before.

Onward, then, ye people, Join our happy throng, Blend with ours your voices in the triumph song;

Glory, laud, and honor, Unto Christ the King; This thro countless ages Men and angels sing.

(chorus) Onward, Christian soldiers, marching as to war, with the cross of Jesus going on before.

Onward Christian Soldiers

As the hymn comes to an end with "This thru countless ages" we can by faith, link arms with the continuous line of brother warriors who have marched "onward" into glory behind the cross of Jesus in their time. In so doing we can resolve to take full measure of our responsibility to join the "happy throng"…join the cadence and get in step marching "onward" in triumph…in our time.

Chazaq v' Amats
(Be strong and of good courage)

—Joshua

Urge all of your men to pray, not alone in church but everywhere. Pray when driving. Pray when fighting. Pray Alone. Pray with others. Pray by night and pray by day. Pray for the cessation of immoderate rains, for good weather for battle. Pray for the defeat of our wicked enemy whose banner is injustice and whose good is oppression. Pray for victory, pray for our army, and pray for peace. We must march together, all for God.

—General George S. Patton
(1885-1945)

Chapter 30

A Warrior's Prayer

Altar Time will Alter You

Almighty, Omnipotent, and loving God. I ask that you give me the courage to face my adversaries, and the skill and strength to fight in the battles which lie ahead. I ask you to superintend over these coming events, and by Your grace, that I will represent you well in the heat of battle. I humbly ask that you, Father God, watch over and comfort my family whom you have given me, while I am engaged in the battles that lie ahead.

Part 6—Songs of War and The Warrior's Prayer

God of Abraham, Isaac and Jacob, I ask that you enable me to be victorious over these evil forces that oppose me and the things of God. I ask that, by your will and purpose, I could be an instrument of your justice and righteousness in the areas you have assigned me to operate. If, in your plan, Precious Lord, I am consumed in the fight, I pray that the sacrifice would be worthy of your name. If I am to prevail, Holy Father, I pray that all would bring glory and honor to you, that the celebration of victory would in every way always be pleasing to You...carefully giving the glory to You!

And when you, Mighty God, have secured the final victory and I can scabbard my sword once again, I will rejoice in You who nurtures and blesses the whole earth and all we to whom you have given life. For all of creation is

A Warrior's Prayer

Yours, in all of its majesty. I pray that in victory I will be humble before you, and will cherish the peace which is found in Jesus Christ alone. I shall rejoice for the food, the water and the air which You provide to sustain me—and for the love of all those You have provided for me to also love and cherish.

In time of peace, my Lord, I ask that in your rich mercy You would keep me from growing soft and cowardly, and that I would be ever vigilant, with my sword always hung in a prominent place and carefully kept—at all times prepared and ready for war!

Part 6—Songs of War and The Warrior's Prayer